# THE DESTINY OF MAN
(c) Copyright 2009
By Earl W. Lacy

All rights reserved. No part of this book may be reproduced, stored in a retrieval system or transmitted in any form or by any means without the prior written permission of the publishers, except by a reviewer who may quote brief passages in a review to be printed in a newspaper, magazine or journal.

ISBN 13: 978-0692670354
ISBN 10: 0692670351

Printed in the United States of America
By: Ecclesia Publishing House LLC

# TABLE OF CONTENTS

| | | |
|---|---|---|
| **INTRODUCTION** | | 3 |
| **CHAPTER ONE** | ELECTION & PREDESTINATION | 4 |
| **CHAPTER TWO** | SPIRIT OF REBELLION | 22 |
| **CHAPTER THREE** | NOT I BUT CHRIST | 36 |
| **CHAPTER FOUR** | THE DESTINY OF MAN | 49 |
| **CHAPTER FIVE** | A NEW SPECIES | 62 |
| **CHAPTER SIX** | THE RESIDENT EVIL | 73 |
| **CHAPTER SEVEN** | CHARMED | 93 |
| **CHAPTER EIGHT** | THE YOKE IS DESTROYED | 108 |
| **CHAPTER NINE** | DELIVERANCE | 116 |
| **CHAPTER TEN** | THE WORLD IS NOT ENOUGH | 125 |
| **CHAPTER ELEVEN** | JEHOVAH-TSKENU | 138 |
| **CHAPTER TWELVE** | SIT, WALK, STAND | 148 |

# INTRODUCTION

What is the *Destiny of Man*? Where do we go from here? The answer to such a profound questions rest in whatever belief system we feel comfortable, whether it's the truth or not. Some believe the Destiny of Man is the grave: The End!

Then there are the Non-Christian Religions and assorted Cults who believe in Reincarnation, the living of successive lives until we finally get right with God; and then there are the Transmigration folks who believe if we live a bad life, we come back as a lower species, perhaps a pig, dog, cat, rat or insect.

Recently on the Science Channel, scientists put forth their theory of the *Destiny of Man*: With the Hubble Space Telescope and Ground-Based Telescopes, they discovered what they termed "Exo-planets" orbiting similar stars such as our Sun. The scientists reached the conclusion there are billions of stars, and each star has at least one planet orbiting it.

With the Next Generation Space Telescope, the James Webb Space Telescope scheduled to launch in 2018, the project represents an international collaboration of seventeen countries led by N.A.S.A, and with contributions from the European Space Agency and the Canadian Space Agency. These scientists believe they will locate Earth-Like Planets; but getting across the enormous distance is the next obstacle.

Now, why all this effort? They believe one day a large asteroid will collide with Earth and cause another Ice age. So if we have another "Earth" to escape to, the Human Race, Man will continue. So, according to the scientists the Destiny of Man is to vacate this world and live someplace else.

Saving Mankind, the Human Race isn't about keeping the Race alive here or on a distant world. Man is more than biological. Our *Divine Destiny* is to be with Jesus Christ, the Messiah.

Let's contemplate who the entity called Man is:

# CHAPTER ONE
## ELECTION AND PREDESTINATION

Moses wrote the first five books of the Old Testament. In the first book of Moses called Genesis, Moses, by inspiration of the Holy Spirit, gave the account of Creation, and the rise and fall of Adam and his descendents. Without the guidance of the Holy Spirit, the Word of Knowledge and the Word of Wisdom which he received, Moses wouldn't have known with certainty the events that transpired before he was born, truths pertaining to the foundation of the world. The Spirit of God was there!

Truth is often stranger than Fiction. The Doctrine of Election and Predestination is difficult to explain and equally difficult to understand; it implies that God had (and still has) a Master Plan; and He's ultimately in control of all Creation; the lives of all Mankind are not in bondage to colliding asteroids, chance—a merciless lottery, fate, luck or probability whose odds are stacked in the house's favor; the odds bent on delivering us at their earliest convenience to the bone yard.

As Christians, our confidence in God's Plans, Purposes and Pursuits isn't as foolish people who daydream their lives away, or those who lean on spider's webs for support--but whose hope is in the Living God. He has a plan that involves *The Destiny of Man*!

> Genesis 1:9, 26 ,28 (King James Version)
> 9 "And out of the ground made the Lord God to grow every tree that is pleasant to the sight, and good for food; the ***Tree of Life*** also in the midst of the garden, and the ***Tree of Knowledge of Good and Evil.*** 26 And God said, Let Us [Father, Son, and Holy Spirit] make Man in Our image, after Our likeness; and let them have ***Dominion over***...all the earth.

Some of the greatest recorded facts in the Holy Bible are within the first few pages. Within the Garden of Eden stood two trees: The *Tree of Life*, and the *Tree of Knowledge of Good and Evil*. The first tree represented the uncreated Life of God called Eternal Life (Elohim/Christ/Holy Spirit). The other tree represented Rebellion, Self-Will, Independence from God, Disobedience and Sin.

God predestined for Adam (which means Man) to confront these issues of life and make a decision. It was God's will for the Trees to be in the Garden; but Adam, created with free will to chose between low he wanted to live out his life.

The enticement, the Iniquity, the desire to do wrong was set before him by Lucifer; but the decision, Adam's right to choose was totally in his control.

The spiritual implications was whether Adam wanted to continue in the Elohim Unity or fellowship with the other spirit (Lucifer) and be acquainted with the knowledge of Good and Evil, become duel- natured in thought and actions.

God created Man in His image, after His likeness. Therefore, God elected and predestinated Adam and his descendents to be like Him. God is a Spirit (John 4:24); Man is a Human Spirit who possesses a Soul and Physical Body). Like God, Adam had Dominion, a kingdom. Adam was the god of the Physical World. Adam radiated with the Glory of God. He had Elohim Life, the Life of God, Eternal--Life that keeps God alive.

Without Elohim Life, God would cease to exist. He is sustained by His Eternal Life, and Adam possessed His Life.

God wouldn't have asked Adam to do what was impossible for him to do. God commanded him to "subdue" the earth (including the Natural and Evil Forces around him). So God brought "every beast of the field, and every fowl of the air; and brought them unto Adam to see what he would call them" (Genesis 2:19).

Adam named everything because he was the king and this was his kingdom. He had the delegated authority and Covenant partnership with God to will and to do according to his pleasure.

God's Election of Grace in choosing an individual or group to perform His will is sovereign. God is the Creator and Man is the steward of His holdings; God is the authorized recipient of the spiritual fruit produced by the stewardship of Mankind.

> Genesis 3:6 (KJV)
> 6 "And when the woman saw that the tree was good for food, and that it was pleasant to the eyes, and a tree to be desired to make one wise, She took of the fruit thereof, and did eat, and gave also unto her husband, and he did eat."

The serpent, the fallen Archangel Lucifer (Ezekiel. 28:14) deceived Eve, and she implemented Adam in the transgression. It was High Treason. The god of this world, Adam now hid from the Presence of the Compassionate One who created and gave him Dominion; the same God who communed and loved him with an everlasting love--he was afraid to face.

God cursed Satan and drew a spiritual line in the sands of the hourglass of time. This enmity line also reached to the highest heavens. Adam made his choice. Of the two trees in the Garden, he chose the Tree of the Knowledge of Good and Evil.

The spiritual line separated God's *Children of Obedience and Faith*---not yet born--- from Satan's and Adam's *Children of Disobedience*, also not yet born.

The prophecy of the "Woman's Seed" ushered in God's **Destiny and Predestinated Plan of Salvation**. God would "legally" win back the Dominion of the Physical and Lower Heavens from Satan and place it back into the rightful hands of His faithful Stewards, His Covenant Partners in governing Creation.

God foreordained that the Woman's Seed, Jesus of Nazareth, the Christ of God would incarnate and crush Satan, dethrone and again subject him to the Obedience and Faith of the Stewards(the Church) of the earth.

The Deceiver who lost his first estate in heaven, whose wi--

cked, diabolical nature was symbolically represented in the Tree of Knowledge, was assimilated into the heart and Consciousness of Adam, the Man. Satan coveted Adam's Stewardship, Kingdom and Dominion and reigned.

But God wasn't caught off guard. God foreknew Lucifer and Adam would rebel against His Authority. God's Authority was typically Balanced, answered with Obedience and Faith. However, with Satan, the Rebel Angels and Adam, God's Authority for the first time met with Rebellion and Disobedience. So Adam forfeited the Title Deed to the Lower Heavens. Satan became the god of mankind,

"It is true that He (Jesus Christ) was *Chosen and Forordained* [destined and foreknown for it] *before the foundation of the world*, but He was brought out to public view [made manifest in chronological time] in these days for the sake of you" (1 Peter 1:20).

God cannot fail; no one can outmaneuver or outthink Him. In a fraction of a second of time He Foreknew, Predestinated and prophesied the end results.

Throughout the generations and the complexity of Human History---and outwitting Satan all the way---God witnessed His obedient Seed, Jesus of Nazareth being born in a stable as a Human Being in the City of David, Bethlehem. At a young age, He saw this Servant respond to His Authority with Obedience and Faith. Then as an Adult, God witnessed Jesus' sinless life, ministry and march to the Cross at Calvary; there Jesus was the *Substitute* for punishment and death for the multitude of sins, sicknesses, offences and reproaches accountable to Mankind, as he unwittingly served in bondage, the Darkness perpetrated by the Devil.

God witnessed Jesus' pain and agony, the Blood fall in great drops to the earth and covered it with Life. God saw the Resurrected Jesus Christ, the High priest of Heaven, carry His Blood into the Heavenly Sanctuary and offer it to Him as payment, Atonement for our sins; then Jesus descended into Sheol (Ephesians 4:9) and become victorious over Satan and the Rulers of Darkness (Colossians 2:15).

His Christ raised from the dead when God exerted His Resurrection Power and again seated Christ at His Right Hand--with the Church, the Redeemed of the Lord, also seated In Him.

God smiled at His new family of Spiritual Children, Regenerated through His Salvation Plan.

According to what God witnessed with His Omniscience, He turned to Satan and declared Himself the victor before Satan even got out of Eden!

> Isaiah 46:9, 10 (KJV)
> 9 "Remember the former things of old: For I AM God, and there is none else; I am God and there is none like Me.
> 10 **Declaring the end from the beginning, and from ancient times that are not yet done, saying My counsel shall stand, and I will do all My pleasure**."

God said it: He's the Alpha and the Omega, the Beginning and the Ending. He calls those things which be not as though they already were. He's Omnipresent (everywhere), Omnipotent (all powerful), and Omniscient (all knowing). He has the Spirit Power and Faith to set into motion Divine Providence, causes that will manifest until His will and pleasure is accomplished.

He manifests to reality things and events that wouldn't naturally evolve by Human effort or random probability. He Creates, Elects and Predestinates according to His Plans, Purposes and Pursuits.

Even so, there are two things God can't do: He can't lie and He can't make us serve Him. He created us by His Free Will and gave us Free Will, so we would be like Him. In everything He desires us to be in His image and after His likeness, not only in Mind, Character, but in Righteousness and Holiness.

Our Free Will often opposes God's Divine Will. Nevertheless God honors our decisions though they may be to our undoing. His perfect will is for us to cooperate, Covenant with Him as Partners to assist in His plans for our life. The problem is we don't is we don't always want or agree with His guidance.

The god of this world has his suction cups and tentacles smack on our world-loving Souls and siphoning the life blood out of our hearts, causing us to sin and fall short of the expectations of God. We're conformed to the world and love it!

God can miraculously change things, and things can naturally change around Him; but God cannot change (Hebrews 13:8). But we can change and be more enlightened; He cannot change because He's already perfect; that which is perfect ceases to become greater or lesser, increase or decrease in any proportion or status--so if change becomes necessary something or someone outside of Him must go through the process. In short, we must experience change to become His Spiritual Children.

God set guidelines, perimeters in His Salvation Plan. "Whosoever will" accept these guidelines will be *Born Again* and conformed to the image of His Son. To "conform" means more than an imitation or a few minor attitude adjustments.

In crucial and supernatural areas, God exercises His Sovereign Will and we have no say; God is a Theocracy and there's no voting, Elections or Corporate Meetings.

For example: God created the heavens, angels, galaxies, earth and Adam without Human cooperation; and God rules His throne and the High Heaven without our consent. His Salvation Plan was set in motion upon His Omniscience, knowing the need for the Human Spirit to again experience Life and Fellowship with Him.

Knowing this, His Divine Grace and Humble, Contrite Spirit motivated Him to rescue His lost Children---because He loved and missed us---and wanted to be our Father again; we were drowning in a sea of Iniquity, filth and degradation; when we are a Royal Priesthood, Joint-Heirs with Jesus Christ.

God foreknowing our need is similar to the way the Police in major cities pick up the homeless when the winter weather becomes extremely cold and hazardous. The homeless, having no radio or television, usually aren't aware of the coming change and imminent danger. Some when warned leave gratefully with the Officers to the Shelter. But others when warned, curse the Police; they don't like the Authorities; some don't care if they live or died; they run, resist and challenge the Authority that gives the Police the right to interfere in their lives.

So God picked us off the streets; we were homeless, in that Heaven being our true home, was inaccessible, and the world being hostile, a burial ground for the flesh--not our real home— God took us out of the cold, warmed and fed us, showered His Love and Protection upon us---but stopped short of forcing us to be Born Again, His Spiritual Children; that was our decision to make. What a mighty God!

> Genesis 25:21,23 (KJV)  Ro. 9:10,11 (Amp. Bible)
> 21 "And Isaac entreated the Lord for his wife ...23 And the Lord said unto her, two nations are in your womb, and *two manner of people* shall be separated from your bowels; and the one people shall be stronger than the other people; and the *elder shall serve the younger.*" 11 "And the children were yet *unborn* and had *so far done nothing either Good or Evil.* Even so, in order further to *carry out God's Purpose of Selection* [election, choice], which depends *not on works or what man can do,* but on *Him who calls* [them]."

God's Salvation Plan was of such future important He Elected, Selected individuals before they were even born. God fulfills His Promises by His Word. He chose ordinary people and delegated to them Leadership abilities: People like Abraham, Isaac, Jacob, Moses, David, Isaiah, He used as instruments, clay vessels to deposit His bountiful treasures of the Holy Spirit to minister to the people whom He loves.

God told Jeremiah: "Before I formed you in the belly I knew you; and before you came forth out of the womb I Sanctified you, and I *ordained you a Prophet* unto the nations" (Jeremiah 1:5). Jeremiah was amazed that God knew him so well. And we need to know God too!

The heartfelt motivation behind God's concern for our well-being is *Agape Love*. "The Lord is...not willing that any should perish, but that all should come to Repentance" (2 Peter 3:9). It's His sincere and *Divine Destiny* (God has a *Destiny* to perform His Word, His Promises and Covenants in Chronological Time, although, He lives in the Present Tense)to fight and win back His Children, to restore us to e our rightful place at His throne, and enjoy our company; and again see us drink from the Living Waters of the Holy Spirit, and learn the Gospel Truth about who He is and who we are; and receive from His outstretched hands the keys to the Kingdom of Heaven.

But we can willfully and foolishly disregard His Rest and Royal Invitation to come, dine at His banquet table and drink out of golden goblets the nectar of the Holy Spirit; we can refuse His offer of Salvation and protection from the "Justice" Scale of His Righteous Indignation, and live whatever wretched, perverse, selfish lifestyle we want to--- die, be Judged and go straight to Hell.

And woe to us if we purposely get in His way when He moves to Save someone else!

> Isaiah 45:9 (Amp. Bible)
> 9 "Woe to him who strives with his Maker!--a worthless piece of broken pottery among other pieces equally worthless [and yet presuming to strive with his Maker]. Shall the clay say to him who fashions it, What do you think you are making? Or, Your work has no handles?"

Man has always questioned God. We challenge His authority. God is the most misunderstood Entity. We blame Him for evil deeds He hasn't done: "Acts of God" we call our calamities--tornadoes, floods, hurricanes and famines which destroy lives and bring sickness and poverty, are attributed to God as though His Spirit Being only resides in the destructive forces of nature. Then we give credit for the blessings and good that happens to a mysical person called "Luck", whom no one ever seen, not even in a vision; or we give the credit to another person, even ourselves. We characterize God as an angry old gizzard who throws uncontrolled tantrums, reeking vengeance and misery upon the Souls who slave in His kingdom.

We're also skeptical about Him because we feel plays favorites---He's unfair in creating us less talented than sister or brother Anointed Teacher: "My handles are missing!" We complain, "I've been discriminated against by the Most High!"

But every creation of God is unique and exist for a special Purpose. God knows what that Purpose is; all we have to do is as Him. It could be that we're working ourselves to exhaustion trying to imitate another's Divine Purpose and not our own.

Many times we're caught up in the Pastor's Vision for his local church---though it may be God-inspired---but God has a different Vision for us outside of that local church. God will provide the labor and finances for that church; sometimes we think we're irreplaceable, or can't be effective or used by God anyplace other than where we are.

Job said, even today is my *complaint rebellious and bitter*; my stroke is heavier than my groan. Oh, that I knew where I might find Him, that I might come even to His seat! I would lay my cause before Him and *fill my mouth with argument*" (Job 23:2-4).

Job wanted to give God a piece of his mind, to tell God off! He believed God had allowed him to suffer and was now hiding from the interrogation Job had waiting for Him. Job filled his mouth with "argument," reasons why he shouldn't suffer loss or be uncomfortable and persecuted in this world.

Job knew he was a righteous man; he believed the righteous shouldn't suffer or experience anything but good. Job lost everything--except his nagging wife.

She blamed him for an unknown sin that offended God. She told him to curse God and let Him put an end to his boil-infested miserable life!

Job 38:4 (Amp. Bible)
4 "Where were you when I laid the foundation of the Earth?"

Job realized the truth. At first Job thought he had a weighty legal argument to present, but now he was speechless. He realized even his thoughts were rebellious. He put his hand over his mouth because he had already said too much. Job's Human reasoning and worldly wisdom motivating him to question God's integrity couldn't compare to God's infinite wonders to perform, miracles of sheer power when He formed the galaxies and wisdom so deep that no man can comprehend--things past finding out.

Job tried to justify himself by the righteousness that he received from God; not knowing that God's imputed righteousness in Man is made perfect through suffering.

The righteous suffer persecution and our lives are not always happy-go-lucky, but it rains on the heads of the righteous and the unrighteous. Suffering isn't a sign of God's approval or disapproval; not even a sign of sin or sinlessness, but a reality, a byproduct of living in this fallen world.

The situation or environment of suffering is often used by the Holy Spirit as a tool to get our attention. We oftentimes overlook valuable lessons in which God wants us to stop and pay attention to: Like driving too fast and miss our exit.

When we suffer what we believe is unjustly we turn to God for answers. In the process we become closer, more intimate with Him. We go as far (in sincerity, not blame or accusations) to ask Him important questions we might not have thought to ask before.

Though we may not want to face it, sometimes we reap what we sowed in word or action; then, also, we reap what someone else, our parents sowed. In any case, Demonic Interference and Curses can be broken from over our lives.

We wait on the Lord, learn Obedience, Patience, Humility. Our Faith is strengthened by our contact with adversity. We become powerful, wise, prepared to assist others who are going through the same or similar tribulations.

God places a Special Anointing on these deep and often painful experiences; people who hear our Testimony, feel that we have apathy, have sat where they sat, and walked in their shoes; this is completely different than someone who only has a Degree, who read in a book about a particular situation, but never experienced it. People can tell the difference. They will open up and talk; and this is the beginning of their way back, their Deliverance and Healing.

Trials and Tribulations makes us more Patient (One of the Fruit of the Spirit, the Characteristic of God). In fact we become more usable, willing to serve and obey God. Then, with this Patience, we better understand and appreciate Christ's suffering on the cross for us, and become more sensitive to the suffering and needs of others. We become better Christians.

Sometimes, like Job, we look for our brand of Justice, a fairness based upon Human Reason and Logic. "That sounds logical!" As Mr. Spock of Star Trek would interject.

Yet God is the True Standard of Justice. He alone has Moral Perfection. His dealings with Creation is just and fair, even if we don't fully understand the wisdom or Standard of Divine Measurement: Jesus Christ is the Divine Standard, the Center of Heaven and Creation.

But, like Job, we can ask God what He is doing but not accuse Him. We inquire of Him for Revelation Knowledge to comprehend what He's doing. We will receive a reply with sufficient Grace to understand because He is well pleased in our asking.

The Prophet Jeremiah was given a message to proclaim: "0 house of Israel, cannot I do with you as this potter does? Says the Lord, behold, as the clay is in the potter's hand, so are you in My hand 0 house of Israel" (Jeremiah 18:6).

God also revealed to Jeremiah this truth: "...in a great house there are not only vessels of gold and silver, but also [utensils] of wood and earthenware, and some for honorable and noble [use] and some for menial and ignoble [use]" (2 Timothy 2:20).

As the heavenly Potter, God has the authority over His Creation. He Elects and Calls some to highly visible ministries, while others to less visible ministries but nonetheless important; some have a greater Measure of Anointing upon them to accomplish the assignment, more supernatural manifestations; nevertheless the Holy Spirit is the One working in each of them.

But, as stated earlier, we have free Will and can chose not to get Saved, or not to serve Him after getting Saved.. Through the exercise of our Free Will we can serve ourselves and knowingly or unknowingly accept Satan to be our god, and assist him to govern his earthly Kingdom of Darkness, sin and corruption; and be a resident of his spacious underworld holdings, on the shores of the Lake of Fire.

We can actively oppose God; we can even become an adversary to the Elect. This is allowed to happen so the Elect can receive experiences through adverse environments, trials, tribulations, hardships, persecutions and even Satanic oppression such as sicknesses, diseases and afflictions--to the end the Elect of God will become strong, and will cleave to, trust and rely totally on God and not the promises of fickle-minded people.

> Romans 9:17, 18 17
> "For the scripture says unto Pharaoh [king of Egypt], even for this purpose *have I raised you up, that I might show My power in you, and that My Name might be declared throughout all the Earth.* 18 Therefore, has *He mercy on whom He will have mercy, and whom He will he hardens.*"

God, to execute His Divine Justice for the individual and national sins of the Egyptian people, displayed His wrath and Righteous Indignation towards Egypt (and other nations) in order to show His Kindness and Generosity towards the Elect. He demonstrated His awesome power and delivered Israel in such a brilliant terror as to establish a Name, an everlasting reputation for Himself that has been remembered throughout History.

What God accomplished in Egypt is still talked about today. Books, even movies have been made and sermons preached about the strength of the Lord God of Israel manifested through His servant, Moses, to Pharaoh: "Let My people go!"

"Let My people go!" Is the same command God gave Satan; but Satan will not heed the voice of God, and he will not let the people go; therefore, he must be FORCED by spiritual violence upon his wretched spirit to submit to the authority of Christ and His Elect. Satan must be rebuked by the Elect, the Church..

"Even so then at this *present time* also is a R*emnant* according to the *Election of Grace*" (Romans 11:5). The Elect was chosen before the foundation of the world. We're called Christians, being the spiritual Children of God. Our names are known and recorded in Heaven; this too was done at the foundation of the world.

Being the Elect, we're Saved by Grace through Faith, Grace being the unmerited favor of God. But our works or potential works weren't even considered in God's wisdom concerning Election.

We didn't send a fax, log an E-Mail, put in a telephone call or fill out an application describing our family tree, education and experience at being a Christian--we were sinners and had no previous Christian existence--in fact, we weren't even born yet when God Called us into the Fellowship with His Son, Jesus Christ.

Therefore, our Salvation is a gift of God; but keeping it takes a conscious effort on our part. Remember, our forgiveness of sins cost Jesus of Nazareth His life. We couldn't afford such a high ransom because we had nothing of eternal value to exchange for our lives: The Blood of Jesus Christ was more than enough.

"For all have sinned, and come short of the Glory of God" (Romans 3:23). This was God's conclusion against Man which led Him to hand down the Indictment. Man was corrupt, and in his mortality, his un-regenerated self, had no redeemable qualities, but Man had spiritual potential. Man was subject to arrest and a

Bench Trial (The Great White Throne Judgment).

"And he showed me a pure River of Life, clear as crystal, proceeding out of the Throne of God and of the Lamb. In the midst of the street of it, and on either side of the river, was there the *Tree of Life*, which bare twelve manner of fruits, and yielded her fruit every month; and the leaves of the trees were for the *healing of the nations*" (Revelation 22:1,2).

We as Christians are God's peculiar treasure, His Workmanship, the results of His Patience and Faith; we are the Remnant separated as partakers of the Tree of Life which thrived magnanimously in the Garden of Eden, with glorious, stellar array, and the fire of Elohim Life surged through its roots, trunk and branched fruit. These Trees represent Christ in the Old and New Testaments.

In the Book of Revelations, was the same River of Life pulsating like a heartbeat flowing majestically into the Physical Realm from beneath God's humble Throne; the two Trees of Life on the banks of the Holy River of Life whose leaves are for the healing of the nations; and surrounding the Throne are Elders, Angels and Saints with their golden crowns cast down before the Lamb.

The Apostle Paul wrote that Christians are the called out ones. "And we know that all things work together for the good of them who love God, to them who are the *Called according to His purpose*" (Romans 8:28). God has foreordained "*all things*" to work together to our advantage; the good, the bad, and the ugly contributes to our spiritual growth and the advancement of the Kingdom of God. **The Destiny of Man is Christ-likeness!**

Christians are a blessed people. We're called according to His Purpose; not to do our own thing but to do His thing. Christ is the Tree and we're the branches. He wills to produce Good Fruit in and through us. These Fruit aren't His last minute efforts to save face before a laughing Devil, but a real yoke-destroying stroke of tenacity to Save a fallen species from the Lake of Fire, the Second Death.

Now Jesus has spiritual heirs to Worship and live in His spiritual Kingdom, sit at His spiritual table, eat and laugh at His spiritual jokes (Jesus Christ is a Person and thus has a personality)--and what a Wedding Celebration and Supper He has prepared for those who love and obey Him!

> Romans 8:29, 30 (Amp. Bible)
> 29 "For those whom He foreknew [of whom He was aware and loved beforehand], He also *destined from the beginning* [foreordained them] to be molded into the image of His Son [and share inwardly His likeness]..."

Again the revelation of Christ brings forth the unfathomable Love God has for us. The complexity of His Person leaves us spellbound and forever thirsting for more.

Before the beginning of Human History God chose of His Free Will certain people, the Elect to receive His gift of Salvation; in that He also *foreknew* at the moment He conceived and knew in His Spirit Consciousness the idea of redeeming Man (whom He hadn't yet created) certain ones in every generation would respond to His Love with Obedience and Faith; and upon those He set His Seal, predestined them to be conformed to the image of His Son. How complex is His Love!

> Ephesians 4, 5 (Amp. Bible)
> 4 "Even as [in His love] *he chose us* [actually picked us out for Himself] in Christ before the foundation of the world, that we should be holy (consecrated and set apart for Him) and blameless in His sight, even above reproach... 5 For He *foreordained us* (destined us, planned in love for us) to be adopted as his own Children through Jesus Christ, in accordance with the purpose of his will [because it pleased Him and was his kind intent]."

For a Christian to deeply understand the workings of God and

His *Agape Love* is part of the ministry of the Holy Spirit. Those who don't have the Holy Spirit can only touch the hem of His garment (which is enough to get Healed or Saved), but not really know Him in their heart.

Our Human Mind staggers to grasp hold of His Plans, Purposes and Pursuits—His goings forth in the Physical Realm. Fortunately for us the Holy Spirit indwells Believers and systematically searches the innermost desires of His heart and reveals the contents to us. It's a fact that God is the ultimate reality and can be known by the regenerated and keen senses of the Born Again Human Spirit.

Our Human Spirit "intuition" can receive and transmit communicative impressions to and from Him. The fact that He continues to be present in our lives supports the conclusion He will finish what He has begun in us.

What is Intuition? In the spiritual sense: The Human Spirit occupied by the Holy Spirit doesn't have to think; it's the Soul and Mind that actually thinks things out through the process of Reasoning. The Human Spirit simply "knows" the solution without having to think and reason it out.

The reason the Human Spirit has "Knowingness" is because God, the Holy Spirit is its Source of Knowledge and Life. So, if our Soul-Mind has a clear channel to our Human Spirit throughout the day, our life would be amazingly different, fruitful and supernatural.

This is also the reason Jesus stated "the Kingdom of Heaven is within us." God sits on the Throne in Heaven; We are seated together, In Him (Christ): and God the Holy Spirit indwells Christians. Our Human Spirit is always in direct contact and presence with God.

Before the foundation of the world God conceived in His consciousness to Save us through Jesus Christ and the Holy Spirit. He willed to Save to the uttermost those who had sank to the gutter-most. He forgave our sins, separated us to live a holy and sanctified life, the life of the New Species of beings. He arranged and decreed: "For by Grace are you Saved through Faith" (Ephesians 2:8). We're God's "works," the Fruit of labor done in His Vineyard. He already planned works for us. We don't have to think up things to do for God. What we have to do is seek His will for our life and obey it!

Ephesians 4:11, 12 (Amp. Bible)
11 "And His gifts were [varied; He Himself Appointed and gave men to us] some to be Apostles (special messengers), some Prophets (inspired preachers and expounders), some Evangelists (Preachers of the Gospel, traveling Missionaries), some Pastors (Shepherds of His flock) and Teachers."

Not only has God predestinated the *Adoption of Children by Jesus Christ and the Holy Spirit*, God also planned works of ministry to be performed in His Name. He Elected certain people to receive Ministry Gifts such as Apostles, Prophets, Evangelists, Pastors and Teachers. It's solely by God's Election of Grace that Church Leaders are chosen.

If God didn't choose us as a Ministry Gift than we are out of place among the Five-Fold Ministry. So the true Church consist of *Foreknown, Predestinated, Called, Elected* and *Foreordained* followers of Christ and Leaders of the Church of Jesus Christ.

Christ, the Messiah has delegated His Authority to the Church; the Ministry Gifts receive a greater measure of the delegated Authority and Spiritual Gifts, then the rest of the body receives a lesser but sufficient measure; yet we all, the "invisible" Church, sit at the Throne of Christ, In Him, and share the Commonalty, the Unity and Oneness of the Spirit.

God "Who hath Saved us, and Called us with a Holy Calling, not according to our works, but according to His own Purpose and Grace, which was given us in Christ Jesus before the world began" (2 Timothy 1:9,11).

Paul wrote that he was "Called and Appointed," and so are

we. The Ministry Gifts, Spiritual Gifts, helps, talents and Anointing are included in our individual Election. Therefore, we must pray that God's will is done in our life. We must also agree with what the Spirit of God reveals to our heart, the Election and Calling--even though it may not be what we wanted—pray the *Prayer of Agreement* that the Calling and gifts will manifest in our life.

"For God's GIFTS AND CALLINGS ARE IRREVOCABLE [He never withdraws them when once they are given, and He does not change His mind about those He gives Grace or to whom He sends His Call]" (Romans 11:29 Amplified Bible).

The King James Version reads that the Gifts and Callings of God are "without Repentance." God doesn't have to repent. He doesn't make any mistakes. He points His finger at us, like the old military recruiting poster: "Uncle Sam wants you!"

So the Ancient One who inhabits Eternity wants to recruit Christian soldiers to help fight the Wars of the Lord.

The Destiny of Man encompasses more than obtaining Knowledge of the world: An American Tourist rode in a boat on the Agusan River in the Philippians.

American to Boatman: "Do you know Biology, Psychology or Geology?"

Boatman: "Sorry Sir, I don't know."

American: "Then you know nothing. You'll die ignorant!"

Later the boat hit a rock and started sinking.

Boatman to American: "Do you know Swimology and Ecapeology from Crocodiology?"

American: "No!"

Boatman smiled: "Well Today Crocodiology will eat your Bodyology, and I will not Helpology, and you will Dieology!"

# CHAPTER TWO
## THE SPIRIT OF REBELLION

The *Destiny of Man* is to get back in good standing with his Creator. When Adam and Eve disobeyed God and partook of the Tree of Knowledge of Good and Evil, they were impregnated, overwhelmed and saturated by the Spirit of Rebellion; it cleaved to their Souls, and instigated lawlessness, contempt and an atmosphere of depravity.

They became *Slaves to Sin* and its consequences. That day the Spirit of Rebellion nurtured the birth of countless iniquities; false idols and the Self-Life being exalted, became the core of being in every un-regenerated Soul Whereas, although Obedience and Faith pleased God (Hebrews 11:6), it was ultimately substituted for Self-Realization, Self-Gratification, Self-Promotion and the "I will" mentality. God's will was not on the list of priorities.

> Exodus 30:8, 9  Leviticus 10:1,2
> 8 And when Aaron lit the lamps at Evening, he shall burn incense upon it, a perpetual incense before the Lord...9 You shall *offer no strange incense thereon*... 1 And Nadab and Abihu, the sons of Aaron, took either of them his censer, and put fire thereon, and put incense thereon, and *offered Strange Fire before the Lord...*
> 2 And there went out fire from the Lord, and devoured them."

The Lord God of Israel gave verbal instructions to Moses, Aaron and his sons concerning the correct procedure to draw near to Him by burning a specific type of incense. Those who desired to approach God must approach Him under His terms, for God is Sanctified and Holy, worthy of Praise and Reverence. He will not be treated like a dog, and tossed a bone.

Before this incident, when Cain offered vegetables from the cursed ground instead of lamb's blood it prompted God to refuse the offering (Genesis 4:5). God won't accept any form of Worship, Offering, Religions, Cults or Philosophies other than what He sanctions.

Thus the **Law of Strange Fire** was introduced to the priests as a shadow of things to come; and disobedience would be likened to the priests offering instead of sheep, goats and bulls, to instead offer pigs, dogs and snakes--these were abominable, unclean, *strange* and therefore unacceptable, rebellious behavior.

Today the same law applies to Mankind. God provided in His Word instructions on how He desires to be worshiped--in Spirit and in Truth (John 4:23). We must not be like Cain who generated his own form of religious worship based upon his estimation of God's worth; or like Aaron's sons who completely disregard God's instructions and offered God handpicked fruit of the flesh.

There's a television commercial advertising a certain type of Whisky. It goes on to say that some of the Whisky, though in Oak Barrels, evaporates; so they call this the "Angels Share"; Then some Whisky soaks in and remains trapped in the Oak Wood of the barrel, and it's called "The Devil's Cut." The point is---God or the Angels have no need for Whisky fumes, so why offer it to Him? Actually, the entire contents of the barrel be-longs to the Devil.

In the past, we may have discovered that we have offended

> 1 Samuel 15:22,23 (Amp Bible)
> 22 "Samuel said, Has the Lord as great a delight in burnt offerings and sacrifices as in obeying the voice of the Lord? Behold, to *obey is better than sacrifice*...23 For *Rebellion is as the sin of Witchcraft*, and *Stubbornness* is as *Idolatry* and *Teraphim* (household good-luck images...

The Lord God considers Rebellion to be the same as Witchcraft. Today, society considers witchcraft an alternate form of worship. We know in part it consists of casting spells, incantations and mixing strange potions. We're told that a Warlock is a Male and a Witch is a Female practitioner. We also reason that only Satan's underlings use such power (the subject of witchcraft is continued in Chapter Seven: *Charmed*).

But God proclaims that Rebellion in any form against Him is practicing Witchcraft; it is the Fruit of the Poisonous Tree, the Tree of Knowledge of Good and Evil is Witchcraft. Not to obey the revealed Commandments and having a defiant, religious and un-teachable heart constitutes witchcraft.

Witchcraft is using the Soul's Self-will and its psychic, mental powers to *Manipulate*, *Intimidate* and *Dominate* someone, or to use the personal will against God in opposition to His revealed Plans, Purposes and Pursuits in this Realm.

Teraphim, household good-luck images are worshipped, cherished and praised for their ability to bring luck; and the worship of self, personalities such as Movie Stars, Music Performers, Athletics etc..and material possessions, instead of worshipping, trusting in and relying on the Lord Jesus Christ; Teraphim is also Witchcraft.

But, sometimes, it's the Celebrity who has the sexually attractive figure or build, the enchanting voice, the magnetic (demonic) personality that draws the worship by their Fans.

Unfortunately, there's witchcraft practiced in the local churches too, because there are many rebellious, self-willed people who cause strife, factions and church splits; there are also members of the local churches who Worship their Pastor more than they Worship Jesus Christ. This too is Teraphim.

To *obey* the Lord Jesus Christ is better than works generated by the mental powers; to obey is to acknowledge, accept and implement the revelation knowledge provided in our Human Spirit. The revelation Knowledge comes from the Holy Spirit. It is God who must prepare the works for our obedience to respond to; all we have to do is agree and do the work. Our own ways aren't necessarily what God wants to do. So we must be sensitive to the prompting of the Holy Spirit within our Human Spirit.

As Humans with a Divine Destiny, an Appointment with the King of Glory, we can't rely upon the flesh.

> Daniel 7:25
> "And he (Satan) shall speak great words against the Most High, and shall wear out the Saints of the Most High."

The carnal nature and the deceptions of the evil forces raging amongst us attempt to trick us into performing an endless cycle of self-initiated works that will not advance the Kingdom of God here on Earth, but are specifically designed by Satan to wear out the saints of God. There is a difference between church work and the work of the Church. One is human effort and the other is God-inspired, sanctioned and empowered works that He can and will accept, because they are His!

To rebel against the Lord's Word is to water our personal Tree of Knowledge of Good and Evil. This Tree is rooted in our heart and must be uprooted and destroyed.

At birth Rebellion is only a seed. As we grow and become more worldly, a deeper indoctrination, the seed matures and takes on roots and a trunk; then branches appear and become strong; then fruit appear on the branches--all the time the world applauds and adores the fruit of our tree. Then when others eat of this fruit, perhaps our children, they too become drunk and out of their minds, corrupted and hardened towards God.

Our children form attitudes and opinions of God from us and become rebellious, thus another generation is born with hearts of stone, making it most difficult for Repentance, and the Holy Spirit to make the change.

Perhaps unintentionally we have produced poisonous fruit; and being led into other forbidden areas through the lust of the flesh, eyes, and the pride of life. This can happen by simply giving place in our hearts to the Devil and Evil Spirits--only God can restore us. The nature of the Soul- Life and flesh is such it cannot be reformed or "churched" into being good; it must experience the cross and be crucified.

> Numbers 12:1,2 (KJV)
> 1 "And Miriam and Aaron spoke against Moses because of the Ethiopian Woman whom he had married...2 And they said, has the Lord indeed spoken only by Moses? Has He not spoken also by us? And the Lord heard it."

Sometimes we bite off more than we can chew. It's the proverbial Foot-In-Mouth Disease. Aaron and Miriam were Moses' biological brother and sister. Aaron was the High Priest and Miriam was gifted as a Prophetess, Praise Leader and Musician. God spoke to them in visions and revelations. Both of them had duties to perform in the Congregation. Apparently it wasn't enough.

Nevertheless, Moses was God's Man, His predestinated Prophet and Leader of Israel. Moses stood between God and Israel. God delegated the Authority and use of His Name to Moses so Moses could perform miracles. Aaron and Miriam were Moses' helpers, yet both of them rebelled against Moses' position of leadership.

God questioned Miriam how it was that she had the nerve to challenge Moses; challenging Moses was a challenge to God. The Black Woman Moses married was his private business and God had no objection to his choice. If Aaron and Miriam had a problem with the marriage they should have brought it up in private separate from the affairs of leadership.

The fact Moses married a Black Woman wasn't the real issue, for God discerned the thoughts and intents of their hearts and revealed it. God exposed them as Rebellious: It was Moses' Leadership Position they wanted. "Has the Lord indeed spoken only by Moses Has he not spoken also to us?" Was to say Moses wasn't the only one capable of leading Israel---we hear from God too; Moses isn't the only righteous and holy one!

At church, we argue over minor differences in opinion. Then we use these differences as reasons to rebel against Church Leadership. We don't like the sermons, music, rules or personalities of the Pastor or maybe only his wife. These things aren't the real issues--no matter where we go or whom is there we can't seem to accept the leaders.

The real issue between Moses' siblings was jealousy; it's the same today. A Church Leader has visibility and influence. The disgruntled couldn't find legitimate fault with Moses' leadership so they criticized his choice of a wife, hoping to stir up strife among the Congregation whereby getting the support of the Princes to demand Moses' resignation.

Rather than face the issues at hand: Our rebellion, envy, jealousy, pride and greed, we generate unhappiness within ourselves and the Congregation, a diversion and smoke screen to hide our real intent, our ambition.

We manipulate the situation and prey on the baby Christians or those unskilled in the Word of God to bring favor and popularity to ourselves. We're fools to scheme, to acquire another's position when God has Predestined that person to be where they are and we to submit and support their ministry. This brand of deviant behavior is also Witchcraft (also Jezebel Spirit) and causes us to be out of sync with God.

The unmerited criticism of Leadership is sometimes subtle but more often malicious; it's not of God but another form of *Strange Fire* offered upon the altar. The real issue might be that we aren't Born Again, our spirit is un-regenerated, or we need to cultivate the Fruit of the Spirit in our lives (Galatians 5:22,23).

> Numbers 16:2, 32 (KJV)
> 2 "And they rose up before Moses, with certain of the Children of Israel, two hundred and fifty Princes of the assembly, famous in the Congregation, men of renown:

32 And the earth opened her mouth, and swallowed them up, and their houses, and all the men that appertained unto Korah."

When Moses was confronted with Korah's Rebellion he fell on his face. It was enough to make a grown man cry. Moses humbled himself before the Lord and his accusers. The aged leader was said to have been the meekest man of his time; in his meekness he truly understood who he was and his place in History---a delegated Authority that no one--not even the "renown" Princes could take from him. He was secure in his personal, intimate relationship with God; his meekness was made perfect by his Faith.

Aaron was also the target of Korah. Now Aaron knew what it was like for someone trying to force him out his position. Previously he and Miriam criticized Moses because of the Black Woman Moses married. They tried to replace Moses. Now the shoe was on the other foot.

Korah and the Princes were rebels. They imitated Satan, who stole the whole world. They accused Moses of hogging all the glory. In effect they said, "who do you think you are? You're no better than the rest of us "famous folks". We're the head of the Twelve tribes of Israel; our families are prosperous and influential, and you put your robe on the same way we do! At this, Moses didn't argue with them. He went to God.

Moses fell on his face and Prayed, Worship and had Church. He had a meeting with God. The decision to stamp out the rebellion came swiftly; Korah, Princes and Congregation immediately knew whom God had put in charge; the opposition was forever silenced. The disease of Rebellion was averted.

Christian Leaders are not Celebrities to be worshipped but respected and obeyed. As long as the leaders are representing Christ, walking in and speaking the Word of God we're required to be in submission to them. It's a hard thing for a Human to submit to another, but the Love of Christ constrain, empowers, and makes it possible. History has revealed---and it's disturbing---how people will readily submit and follow a stone-cold lunatic but not a true representative of God!

Our Christian Leaders aren't perfect and neither are we as followers; they aren't infallible but flesh and blood servants who watch over our Souls, and are often viciously attacked by the evil spirits for doing so.

Nevertheless, whomever the Leadership Anointing is upon, as with Moses, God's Seal of Approval is with them also. As followers we can share in the Leadership Anointing until we receive our own; this is done by working with someone who already has the Anointing. By helping their ministry flow orderly, or even carrying their books as an Armor Bearer, we share in their reward (1 Samuel 30:24).

> Ezekiel 2:3 (KJV)
> 3 "And He said unto me, Son of man, I *send* you to the Children of Israel to a Rebellious nation ...

God anointed the Prophet Ezekiel as His delegated Authority to the Children of Israel. The indictment God presented against the Elect was that Israel was *Rebellious, Impudent* and *Stiff-Hearted*. He also described them as briars, thorns and scorpions. They wouldn't accept correction. But in the depths of His compassion he sent Ezekiel to them.

God knew Rebellion was like a contagious disease. He knew Rebellion sprang from the self-will of His people,

Therefore, He warned Ezekiel to be careful in his associations with the Congregation. The Spirit of Rebellion, being Witchcraft, was subtle but had the sting of a scorpion. He didn't want Ezekiel to become a victim, whereas a Rebellious prophet was of no use to Him; he would only frustrate the Master's plans.

Jesus Christ came to the Rebellious Israel and a heathen world. His own people didn't receive Him or believe on His Name. The

Word of God He brought was sweet to those whose hope was in Obedience but sour to those on the path of Disobedience.

Even today the Word of God affects the masses the same way. Some embrace the Word because of necessity and an inner conviction to get right with God; others flee from the Word and the Light of Christ because of His life-changing Spirit that discerns the condition of the Soul and brings conviction of sin.

The Holy Spirit also brings convincing of Righteousness and Judgment. Many cannot stand the scrutiny of their sinful lifestyles being viewed under His microscope. They flee from the Word.

But sinners must be warned of the consequences of their wickedness and pending Eternal Judgment. Therefore, does the Lord of the Harvest send labors into Creation because the harvest is plenteous but the labors are few, and the Rebellious must be presented the Word of God, given the opportunity to get aboard their *Destiny* before this ship sails away without them.

The Rebellious looked upon Jesus' outer appearance and didn't think He fitted the profile of a Spiritual Leader. Many saw a thirty-year-old carpenter's son with big ideas and a vivid imagination. They justified not listening to Him by conveniently and systematically dismissing, minimizing His importance and claims to Divine Authority.

We do the same thing to Him and to His servants, looking for faults--no matter how absurd or insignificant, and conclude that God isn't using them, dismissing ourselves from being Obedient.

Again, Rebellion against God's Anointed is Rebellion against God the Person. True, Church Leaders must live Holy and Sanctified lives, continuously be available to the Holy Spirit, but so does the general Congregation. The truth is we often expect our leaders to live blamelessly but we live according to what we feel is right in our own eyes. Shame on us!

Our focus isn't to work out our *own* Salvation with the help of the Holy Spirit, but to monitor the lifestyle of the leadership; we take upon ourselves a false "overseer" ministry.

Jonah 1:1-3 (KJV)
1 "Now the Word of the Lord came to Jonah... 2 Arise, go to Nineveh, that great city, and cry against it; for their wickedness is come before Me. 3 But Jonah rose up to flee from the Presence of the Lord, and went to Joppa..."

The Prophet Jonah rebelled and fled from the Presence of the Lord. Jonah hated the Assyrians. He actually wanted God to wipe them off the face of the Earth. Jonah allowed his personal feelings, opinions to affect his judgment and prophetic ministry. Ultimately, his disobedience landed him in the stomach of a large fish. He was inside the fish three days and three nights. Only his Repentance and fervent prayers saved him.

The story of Jonah is a classic example of the Mercy and restoring Grace the Father offers to those who rebel, seek Forgiveness and find it through Repentance, a reversal of direction.

Walking in the Spirit and winning Souls is the Wisdom of the Most High. God's Elect have the Commission to win the lost Souls.

God said: "Let him know, that he which *covers* the Sinner from the error of his ways shall save a soul from death and shall hide a multitude of sins" (James 5:20).

Jonah was to "cry against", rebuke and warn the Assyrians for their wicked ways. Instead, the Prophet was rebuked by God for his wicked ways; the Mercy God is deep: He's not willing that anyone should perish--including those whom Jonah despised.

We too must be careful as not to neglect the spiritual welfare of those we don't particularly care to be around. It will come to pass that they might be the first ones God sends us to.

Jesus Christ is our example of Obedience. He answered God's Authority with a "Yes," unwavering Obedience. Jesus accomplished what Adam failed to do. "For by one man's [Adam's] Disobedience many were made Sinners, so by the Obedience of One [Jesus Christ] shall many be made Righteous.

As stated previously, Adam forfeited the Title Deed to the world. His disobedience caused Sin and Death symbolically represeted in the Tree of Knowledge of Good and Evil to seize his Spirit, Soul, and Body. Thereafter through the Male Blood, his X Chromosome, Adam's descendants weren't created in the Spirit Image of God, but after Adam's fallen Human State and likeness thereof; and the image of the Prince of Darkness. Sin, sickness and death reigned because of and by way of the Sin of Rebellion.

But Christ incarnated to destroy the works of the Devil and the Fruit of the poisonous Tree. God's righteousness will always prevail, and His Word will never fall to the earth unfulfilled.

> Heb. 5:8 (KJV)
> 8 Though He was a Son (Jesus of Nazareth), yet *learned He Obedience by the things which He suffered...*"

By the aid of the Holy Spirit, the Apostle Paul wrote many passages describing the Obedient life of Jesus. He suffered and obeyed in consideration of the larger Plan, the "bringing *many sons unto glory*, to make the Captain of their Salvation perfect through suffering."

No one wants to suffer; but Jesus of Nazareth suffered not only on the cross, but once He was draped with the cloak of misery, the flesh, he endured Human Family Life. He had trials and tribulations---His Stepfather, Joseph died and Mary was so in love with that man; so Jesus comforted Mary and endured the sting of death in His close-knit family.

> Ephesians 2:1-3
> "And you has He quickened (made alive), who were dead in trespasses and sins: wherein in time past you walked according to the course of the world, according to the Prince of the Power of the Air, the [evil] spirit that works in the Children of Disobedience."

That "spirit" is the Spirit of Rebellion; it works in the heart of

Man as Disobedience to the revealed Word of God.

In the end, after the fact, Adam learned Obedience by suffering the consequences of his Disobedience. The Prophets and Israel attended the school of hard knocks--bumped their heads against the stone walls of life, being thrown in dungeons and captiveities, then being crushed by the slow moving wheel of time.

But Jesus of Nazareth learned Obedience by the Trials and Temptations He faced and overcame through Faith in the Word and Salvation Plan of God.

Early in His life He agreed in His entire being not to do His will, be pressured into conforming to society, or the expectations of relatives and friends (unlike King Saul who was "afraid of the people" and disobeyed God), but to perform the will of Jehovah-Elohim who Called and sent Him forth.

His victory over Sin and the Death on the cross answered the Call and fulfilled the Obedience expected by the Father from all mankind. As His reward the Father highly exalted Jesus and gave Him the Name (Reputation) that is above all other names (reputations); Philippians 2:9). In response to the Exceeding Greatness of this Name, ever knee shall bow and every tongue confess that Jesus Christ is the Lord!

As the Elect, predestined to be with the Lord, we often suffer in order to learn not to be Rebellious or Disobedient to His Word. We suffer the consequences, reciprocity--the Law of Sowing and Reaping--for our actions.

Yet suffering, as in the case of Job, and sickness aren't always contributed to personal sin. More often the manifestation of pain is a sign of imbalances within the Natural Body or Soul-Mind; suffering and sickness can be a warning, a wakeup call that we're out of sync with the Holy Spirit within us.

Suffering, the in the case of Christians, focuses our attention on God. He may wish to speak to us concerning our lifestyles and attitudes, but we ignore him and even the advice of doctors concerning our High Blood Pressure; then we get sick or hospitalized: Now we're ready to listen!

Matthew 21:28-31 (KJV)

28 "But what think you? A certain man had two sons; and he came to the first, and said, Son, go today in my vineyard. 29 he answered and said, I will not; but afterward he repented, and went. 30 And he came to the second, and said likewise. And he answered and said, I will go; and went not. 31 whether of them did the will of his father? They say unto Him, the first. Jesus says unto them, Verily I say unto you. That the publicans and the harlots go into the Kingdom of God before you."

Jesus had many hard lessons to teach Israel. He came unto His own people, the Jews, and they didn't receive Him. The religious order of His day weren't much different than the "religious" order of today.

The *religious group* is more interested in looking spiritual. We must not be more interested in rituals and commandments of men or going through the motions than obeying the Spirit of God. We shouldn't say, "use me Lord; here I am, I will go," and don't.

As Christian Leaders we shouldn't depend solely our Theological Degrees, aerobic lectures, "whooping and hollering" and other religious gymnastics whose purpose is to impress men; these works aren't authentic, Holy Spirit inspired.

Knowledge of God is gained in many ways: It's gained by listening to preaching, attending Bible Study, Seminary and direct Revelation from the Holy Spirit. A diploma or degree may be issued on the completion of a Bible Course. But it's actually the Holy Spirit who bears witness to the knowledge and gives us the Confidence, will to believe the doctrines are true.

The Authority to represent God doesn't come from man; the Authority, Calling and Anointing comes from the Holy Spirit. Through Revelation Knowledge the Holy Spirit is capable of teaching us without "formal" schooling; yet Jesus through the Holy Spirit gave the Church Apostles, Prophets, Evangelists, Pastors and Teacher, to edify, build us the Body of Christ, including present and future Leaders.

During the Ministry of Jesus, the Sanhedrin Council consisted of Pharisees and Sadducees who were the religious authority in Israel. These men were the "experts" on the Word of God, but not doers of it. They were self-righteous, proud and didn't advance the Kingdom of God an inch---but advanced corruption in their own material kingdom, which amounted to advancing the influence of the Tree of Knowledge of Good and Evil. Because of that, sin reigned in them and they were Rebellious, defiant to Moral and spiritual change.

These things were written for us so we don't make the same mistakes that the Elect, the Children of Israel or the Early Christian Church Members made.

The history and struggles of the Elect from the foundation of the world should supply us with basic knowledge and understand of God and His dealings with Man.

There need no ghost come from the grave to tell us this!
The Lord Jesus Christ is the Center of Heaven and Creation. He is Head of the Church: Father/Son-Church/Holy Spirit. And it's the Holy Spirit who is the Commonalty which binds the unity together; The Holy Spirit is Eternal Life.

When Jesus ascended He sent back the Holy Spirit; the Holy Spirit is also God whereby He has the gifts to give and does give them to the Earthbound Church Members for the "perfecting of the saints" (Ephesians 4:11,12). Those Elect Leaders have a greater responsibility. To rebel against them would only make their ministry more difficult; but to grieve the Holy Spirit would make our lives most miserable!

# CHAPTER THREE
## NOT I BUT CHRIST

In the previous Chapters we shared where the Root, the Foundation of Rebellion and Disobedience originated. In the Tree of Knowledge of Good and Evil, Man sought refuge in self-expression and *will worship*, the soul-life. The Tree of Life had become off limits to Adam and Eve and their descendants. Jesus Christ came to change all that. He came to take back what the Devil stole, granting Man access to Eternal Life, Christ Within, not the symbolic Tree.

> Isaiah 53:4, 5 (Amp. Bible)
> 5 But He was wounded for our transgressions, He was bruised for our guilt and iniquities; the chastisement [needed to obtain] peace and well-being for us was upon Him, and with the stripes [that wounded] Him we are Healed and made whole."

The Prophet Isaiah saw Jesus in a vision six hundred years before the event, the crucified Jesus of Nazareth, the Son of Jehovah-Elohim. God sent His beloved Son into the world to become a Human sacrifice. Jesus sacrificed His Human Spirit Body to annul the curse of Adam's Sin, which brought Spiritual Death.

His Physical Body was sacrificed for every physical Sickness and Disease. He sacrificed His Soul Body, the Soul-Life of His individuality, the "I" Psyche/Mind (consisting of the Intellect, Emotions, Imagination, and Will) for the Mental Illnesses, Sins and Iniquities of the Human Mind.

God's Authority, Righteousness and Justice was appeased by all three offerings. Through these offerings, as God Healed and raised Jesus of Nazareth from the dead: Spirit, Soul, and Physical

Body, to *Glorification*--- we will one day receive the same Resurrection and Glorification.

The Father, through the Holy Spirit accepted Jesus' offering not to cover but to eliminate our Past, Present and Future sins. The Crucifixion of Jesus Christ was also to signify how corrupt the flesh of Man really was; and the reality the flesh cannot please God, neither the mind of Man and subsequent actions of Man.

But the Resurrected New Creation Human Spirit can please Him; in that Christ can please, satisfy and fellowship with God. The Spirit of Christ within us can live the Christian lifestyle. We're Declared Righteous through the Lord Jesus Christ.

This fact led Paul to write, "I am crucified with Christ: nevertheless I live; yet not I but Christ lives in me; and the life I now live in the flesh I live by the Faith of the Son of God, who loved me, and gave Himself for me" (Galatians 2:20).

Herein lies the Mystery of living the victorious life. Not that we continue to live in the Soul-Life of our own strength, but in the victorious Resurrected Life of Christ in us.

Therefore, "Christ has redeemed us from the Curse of the Law, being made a Curse for us: for it is written, cursed is everyone that hangs on a tree (Deuteronomy 21:23): that the blessings of Abraham might come on the Gentiles through Jesus Christ" (Galatians 3:13,14).

We're blessed (happy, and to be envied), having been Redeemed from the Curse of the Law of Sin and Death.

Jesus made it possible for us to live by a higher law, the ***Law of the Spirit of Life***. He conferred upon us His victory over Sin and Death, an imputed righteousness through Faith in His Name. He brought the Crucified Life, living by the Fruit of the Tree of Life; not living by the life of the flesh or the Soul-Life but the Elohim- Life of Christ within.

Because of our relationship and sharing of His victory at Calvary we are "buried with Him in Baptism, wherein also you are risen with Him through the Faith of the operation of God, who has raised Him from the dead. Blotting out the handwriting of

Ordinances that were against us, which was contrary to us, and took it out of the way, nailing it to the cross" (Colossians 2:12,14).

Jesus said, "Think not that I am come to *destroy* (abolish) the [Mosaic] Law, or [abolish the prophesies of] the Prophets: I am not come to destroy, but to *fulfill*" (Matthew 5:17).

Jesus Christ fulfilled the Spiritual, Righteous, Legal, Letter and Moral requirements of the Mosaic Law. He answered the Father's Authority with Obedience for the Species called Man.

Jesus made it possible for us to have a choice whether to live under the Old Testament Covenant: Mosaic Law (of *Sin and Death*) or the New Testament Covenant: The *Law of the Spirit of Life*.

For "...no man is Justified [declared not guilty] by the Law in the sight of God, it is evident: For the Just (Justified) shall live by Faith" (Galatians 3:11).

"For since by Man came Death, by Man came also the Resurrection of the Dead. for in Adam all die, even so In Christ shall all be made alive" (1 Corinthians 15:21,22).

Since the Holy Spirit of God has brought us near into the Family of God, we're obligated to allow the *Law of the Spirit* to govern us. And since the *Law of the Spirit* is the higher Law, the perimeters in which God lives by, it stands to reason that since He overcomes we'll overcome too.

Through the *Law of the Spirit of Life*, the Spiritual Gifts and Fruit of the Spirit operate. The old Law, ruling over the Un-Regenerated Man, the Sinner is "buried with Him in Baptism". The New Man, Resurrected in Christ's image is raised through the Faith in the operation of God; and the *Law of the Spirit*, based upon *Agape Love* nailed the Mosaic Law and its Ordinances to the cross where it belongs.

Under the Mosaic Law: "As it is written, There is NONE RIGHTEOUS, NO NOT ONE" (Romans 3:10). Now God has given us His Righteousness in exchange for our Repentance of Sins, Faith and Obedience to the Word of God.

But if we believe that we have no sin we declare that His Indictment against us is a False Accusation. But it's actually the Mosaic Law that convicts us of Sin. "Now we know that what things whatsoever the Law says, it says to them who are under the Law: that every mouth may be stopped, and all the world may become Guilty before God. Therefore by the deeds of the law [sin and death] there shall no flesh be Justified in His sight."

The way around this Law of Sin and Death is the Law of the Spirit of Life in Christ:

> Galatians 5:16,18 (Amp. Bible)
> 16 "But I say, walk and live [habitually] in the [Holy] Spirit [responsive to and controlled and guided by the Spirit]; then you will certainly not gratify the cravings and desires of the flesh (of human nature without god). 18 but if you are guided [led] by the [holy] Spirit, you are not subject to the Law."

Getting out from under the Law of Sin and Death is the first priority of Man who wants his *Destiny* to be more than the grave and Hell. Unless this Law is superseded in our life by the *Law of the Spirit of Life* there will be no change in our *Destiny*.

The battle over the Human Soul is Eternally settled by whomever we obey as Master: God and His Spirit or Satan and the Law of Sin and Death.

We must consistently identify with God and His Program. Again we must "*habitually*" walk in the Spirit, having an "addiction" to God and letting the Holy Spirit direct us. The "antagonistic" old nature must be brought under the supervision of the Holy Spirit, otherwise we'll be prevented from serving God to our fullest potential, and not as many souls will be introduced to the Kingdom of God through our witness.

Some of the works of the flesh are: Impure thoughts, lust, hatred, racism, violence, jealousy, manipulation, intimidation, domination,

Selfishness, complaining, rebellion, strife, criticism, conceit, pride, envy, idolatry, spiritism, drunkenness, cheating, adultery, homosexuality, greed, stealing, lying, perversion and worldliness (many of these are listed in Galatians 5:19-21).

"But the Fruit of the Spirit is Love, Joy, Peace, Longsuffering, Gentleness, Goodness, Faith, Meekness, Temperance: Against such there is no law... and they that are Christ's have crucified the flesh with the affections and lusts" (Galatians 5:22-24).

The difference between the two Laws is the difference between Night and Day. In the physical darkness we can see when our eyes conform (adjust) to the environment; but the light is more glorious and it impacts the senses and generates warmth like the light and warmth of the Sun. But the darkness, the shadow has no brilliance; it's but the absence of light. So God's Spirit makes walking in this world safer and blessed as we discern more clearly to avoid the pitfalls, traps and snares left by Satan.

People asked Jesus an important question: "...what shall we do, that we might work the works of God? Jesus answered and said unto them, this is the work of God, that you Believe on Him whom he has sent" (John 6:28, 29).

The people asked in sincerity how they could do God's work. It appeared that Jesus sidestepped the question when in fact he revealed more than most are willing to accept.

The truth being that we as Human Beings cannot do God's work or the work of God; No one but God can do the work of God! Jesus tells us that by believing on His Name, the Holy Spirit is received, and since the Holy Spirit is God---He does the works of God. God's works are done by the partnership of the Son and Holy Spirit operating within the perimeters of the *Law of the Spirit of Life*.

Therefore, works not initiated by God originated somewhere else and belong to the flesh or the Demonic Kingdom. Again, God doesn't accept Human works and credit them to our account apart from the Holy Spirit initiating and manifesting them through us.

Our works are tainted with hidden motives, agendas; they are selfish, Soul-Life and not at all spiritual. Because God is Spirit, His works are spiritual and supernatural. If the Father, Son or Holy Spirit spoke to us we witnessed a miracle.

But it pleases to God to do His works through Man. His communication goes from Holy Spirit too Human Spirit. The nature of the mind is so corrupt Jesus had to die to Justify us remaining alive on Earth. In consideration of that, the mind isn't a reliable avenue for God to trust His works to. The mind is subject to emotions, distortions and Demonic Interference, therefore God uses the "Christ In Us" (Colossians 1:27) who is the *Real Christian; "Not I but Christ..."*

Jesus Christ is the ORIGINAL CHRISTIAN, and with *Christ In Us* we live the wonderful lifestyle in the Holy Spirit and allow the *Christ In Us* to work the works of God. He's the only one who has and continues to please the Father.

Many times we fail as Christians not being instructed in the beginning of our walk how necessary it is to walk by Faith. We're not taught the Full Gospel, the reality of Jesus' and our crucifixion and the provisions of the Cross. Then we fail to assimilate the Wisdom, appropriate the *Full Gospel* that it's *Christ In Us* who's supposed to live and work the works of God.

We struggle to please God, to live Holy and righteously, to "manufacture" good works through our Soul-Life (Mental Life Powers); we use the corporal body and its life (bios) as an instrument to render works for God; but we aren't informed that godly works are inclusive of the Life of the Spirit.

Now in our Christian walk, we must learn to get self out of the way and let Christ live his extraordinary Christian Life in and through us to win souls into the Kingdom of God.

The Apostle Paul wrote: "for we are His workmanship, created in Christ Jesus unto good works, which God has before ordained that we should walk in them" (Ephesians 2:10). We're God's "works", the Fruit of His centuries-old Salvation Plan. The only works we can do for God are those He foreordained and initiated through Christ. And it starts and ends with, as Jesus told the crowd, "Believing on His Name." The rest should be the work of Christ In us."

> Romans 6:3-6 (Amp. Bible)
> 3 "Are you ignorant of the fact that all of us who have been baptized into Christ Jesus were Baptized into His death? 4 We were buried therefore with Him by the Baptism into his death, so just as Christ was raised from the dead by the glorious [power] of the Father, so we too might [habitually] live and behave in newness of life.

Christians are forever spiritually and symbolically connected to Jesus Christ and His sacrifice on the Cross of Calvary. His Death has became our Death; His Life our Life. Water Baptism symbolically represents the Death, Burial, and Resurrection of Jesus Christ. Baptism isn't just an outward sign of an inward change--a catchy phrase--it also confirms our Death at the Cross; it's our sharing in His suffering unto death and reaping His Resurrection.

But it's through the vehicle of Faith that we accept having been Crucified. We accept as truth the Holy Scriptures and allow the Cross of Jesus Christ to work Death in our old selves---until we lose the insane love for the world, and all that remains is Obedience and Faith *In Christ*; when all is peaceful, tranquil inside, the Resurrection Lifestyle will be the sole survivor because it's the ultimate reality, stronger than the love of the world.

Experimentally, if the Physical Body (and its bios life), Soul Body (and its psyche life) are Crucified the only Body left is the Spirit Body which houses the Holy Spirit.

We being Crucified with Christ and raise from the dead isn't a future event (like the Second Advent or Rapture of the Church) but a past reality, engraved in the ancient heavenly scrolls before Creation.

The Crucifixion and Resurrection Power can be claimed! Remember, "they that are Christ's have Crucified the flesh..."

(Galatians 5:24). It only a matter of "Reckoning," considering, claiming the Crucifixion and Resurrection that followed.

A Psychiatrist may argue that considering oneself as dead is called Cotard Syndrome, also called Walking Corpse Syndrome; a rare Mental Illness in which an afflicted person has the delusion that they are dead. This person actually stops eating, hygiene, and other things healthy people do. Eventually they die of complications stemming from Malnutrition or Starvation.

However, we are not talking about denying that we exist, but separating ourselves, ceasing from the sinful acts of the flesh. Of course we eat, exercise, go to work, love and take care of our family and selves; our Physical Body is the Temple, the vehicle our Soul, Human Spirit and Holy Spirit uses to communicate with the people living n the world.

Then why do Christians sin? Why do we "miss the mark" and sometimes cannot be distinguished from the world? The answer lies in us not allowing the Death of the Cross to make "ineffective and inactive" the *Psyche and Mental Powers* of our Soul and Mind. This causes the Life of the Spirit to be silent while the other two *Powers* rule our entire being. We fail to Walk and Live in the Spirit; we struggle against the Law of Sin and Death and sometimes give in to them.

Faith in the Word of God should bring us to realize all the above things; that we have been crucified over two thousand years ago. We fight against the Law of Sin when in fact the battle isn't ours but the Lord's; and He has already gotten the victory. He now waits upon us to enforce that victory through the Authority of the Believer in Christ Jesus.

We're like a drowning swimmer fighting the waves of the turbulent sea. The more we fight the more we have to fight to stay above the waves. Our fighting doesn't diminish the strength of the sea but it does diminish our strength; nor can we wrestle the sea into submission. But if we relax our mind and body, lay on our backs and float, we can survive until help comes.

Living the Crucified Life isn't a once in a lifetime decision, that decision, that when we agree it's done. Living this life involves a daily commitment of Walking in the Spirit. Jesus commented on this lifestyle: "And He said unto them all, If any man will come after Me, let him deny himself, and take up his Cross, *daily,* and follow Me" (Luke 9:23).

He said this before He went to the Cross. He knew of His pending Crucifixion and the Resurrection Power that would be released and available through Faith to whosoever, after denying himself would travel the Calvary Road, and be freed from the slavery of the Law of Sin and Death. As the Great Physician, taking up our Cross daily was His prescription for our chronic sinfulness: Jesus makes house calls!

"Christ our life" (Colossians 3:4) and "For me to live is Christ, and to die is gain" (Philippians 1:21), is how Paul summed it up. A life centered around Christ and not the "I" is a life of victory. To know Him is to share in all He is.

The thought of Death may seem extreme, at the least, repulsive. That's because our minds rebel at the very idea of losing control; Death sounds so hopeless, final and shrouded in mystery. The Death we as Christians embrace only pertains to making ineffective and impotent the Law of Sin and death working in our members, getting us in trouble with God.

But Apostle Paul tells of his great longing "that I may win Christ...That I may know Him, and the Power of His Resurrection and the fellowship of His suffering...if I might attain the Resurrection of the Dead" (Philippians 3:10,11).

In Paul's Missionary Journeys, some may have thought Paul was mad for wanting to experience someone else's Death! Why would he desire to know this suffering? Paul knew that by knowing and experiencing such a death, he would come into the knowledge and operation of the Holy Spirit in the Resurrection.

Paul wasn't seeking this information in order to permanently translate into Heaven, or to tap into Psychic Power, but to assimilate, to experience the moment the Commandment of God went forth; when God exerted His power and raised Jesus from the dead. Paul wanted to live on Earth in that moment and state of Christ's Resurrection and Awareness.

> Romans 7:4 (Amp. Bible)
> 4 "Likewise, my brethren, you have undergone death as to the Law through the [crucified] body of Christ, so that now you may belong to another, to Him Who was raised from the dead in order that we may bear fruit for God."

Again the Scriptures confirm that we're Crucified with Christ and by His Death we're released from the Authority of the Mosaic Law. Like Physical Death releases us from the Marriage Vow, so we're released from Sin by means of *"reckoning ourselves as Dead"* When we were Crucified, experimentally we died to the Old Life and were "Married" to Christ. We went from Buried to Married!

Our Mental Life Powers, once centered on self are now centered on the Cross, put to Death, then the Spirit of Christ ministers through our Soul to accomplish His will and works. Our whole way of living and interacting with the world changes;

The "*motions of sins*" are the sinful passions aroused by the Law of Sin and Death. When this Law stated "you shall not..." our old nature said "why can't I still do that? Who will stop me? The pleasure is worth the punishment." The Old Nature will rationalize and justify itself until satisfied that it's okay to sin.

> Romans 7:14-18 (Amp. Bible)
> 14 "We know that the Law is Spiritual; but I am a creature of the flesh [carnal, unspiritual], having been sold [by Adam] under [the control of Sin. 15 For I do not understand my own actions [I am baffled, bewildered]. I do not practice or accomplish what I wish, but I do the very thing that I loathe [which my moral instincts condemn]."

Just imagine a Christian Minister walks down the street on a on a sunny day. He cast a shadow because the sun is behind him. So he decided to play a little game to pass the time. He lifts his arm but his shadow lifts its leg; he lifts his leg but his shadow lifts its arm. Dumbfounded, the Pastor claps his hands but his shadow does nothing. The Pastor stops in his tracks but his shadow keeps going. When he reaches his home his shadow is already there, sitting on the steps. He's shock to see his shadow smoking a cigar and drinking beer; behaviors the Pastor gave up years ago.

The Pastor calls his wife. She comes out and throws her arms around him because she's happy to see him. He thinks to say to her, "I love you;" but his shadow blurts, "I hate you and want a divorce!" Then her shadow gets offended and slaps the taste out of the man's mouth. Her shadow says, "I think Deacon Fry would be me a better lover than you anyway!"

The above story sound preposterous but the shadow represents the Rebellious part of Man, a part that can and does oppose the desires of the real person.

Apostle Paul wrote to the Christians concerning the battlefield within the Mind, the two opposing Laws waging war in every Christian who wants to live Holy. Although we know what's morally right we still do what's wrong.

It seems there's another "person" inside us. In reality the conflict is the **Sin Principle** (providing we don't have an indwelling Unclean Spirit) not allowing us practice what we know is righteous living. This *Sin Principle* must be overcome before we can walk in integrity.

"0 wretched man!" Was the cry of Apostle Paul, and many veteran Christians alike. The inward struggle against Sin and the burden of trying to live Holy has driven Christians to despair, even away from Christianity. Once it's realized what Christianity requires, trying to dot every "I" and cross every "T" seems impossible.

We find ourselves in the middle of the war between the Flesh and Spirit. We struggle for a time then give up. We attempt to annihilate that Law of Sin by shear will power; and try to please God using our Mental Facilities. But we've underestimated the strength of Sin: we cannot destroy, overcome a Spiritual Law with willpower. But a higher Law can supersede it.

Remember, there were two Trees in the Garden of Eden representing two Laws; the Free Will of Adam (Man) could ONLY decide between which Law to follow, and leave the other intact. The will has no power to destroy either Law.

However, the tremendous power of Christ, working under the *Law of the Spirit of Life*, can supersede the influence of the *Law of Sin and Death.* Through Faith in our Crucifixion with Christ we experience success against the Flesh, plus Deliverance from Unclean Spirits that may be hindering our progress.

Living the Crucified Lifestyle, Walking and Living in the Spirit frees us from Condemnation (Romans 8:1). We aren't adjudged Guilty of Sin if we walk in the *Law of the Spirit*.

The *Law of the Spirit* has freed us from the *Law of Sin and Death*. God, through the Holy Spirit has done what we couldn't do ourselves. Our entire nature without the Holy Spirit is beggarly. But Jesus Christ condemned not us but Sin operating in our flesh. He subdued and overcame gloriously through His Spirit; He deprived Sin of its power to control us as Christians.

Christ through the Holy Spirit fulfilled for us all the righteous requirements of the Mosaic Law. Now the Holy Spirit continues to operate within the perimeters of the *Law of the Spirit of Life.*

The Holy Spirit diligently watches over our thought stream day and night. He checks and reveals to us our unholy desires to gratify the flesh. "Because the mind of the flesh [with its carnal thoughts and purposes) is hostile to God, for it does not submit itself to God's Law; indeed it cannot" (Romans 8:7).

Life in the Spirit is the only choice we have to escape the living in the iniquity of our minds. "For all who are led by the Spirit of God [the Holy Spirit] are Sons of God. For [the Spirit which] you have received [is] not a Spirit of slavery to put you once more in bondage to Fear, but you have received the Spirit of *Adoption* [the

Spirit producing Sonship] in [the ]bliss of] which we cry Abba (Father)! Father! The Spirit Himself [thus] testifies together with our [Human] Spirit [assuring us] that we are Children of God" (Romans 8:14-16).

The *Spirit of Life* is the power behind the New Birth. The Holy Spirit, living by the Eternal Spiritual Law, the *Law of the Spirit* is the One who Adopted and placed us in the Father's family. Now we can consciously choose to allow the Spirit of God to live and express Himself in us every day, and impact the environment in which we live. So we must consciously center our lives on God and His Program. When the Spirit directs us we must spring into action.

In times of war, the siren shrieks a warning before the enemy planes arrive to drop their bombs. Our Military scrambles to their planes and posts to defend the Base. So it is with the Holy Spirit: He sounds the alarm when our thoughts get dangerous (a Cause) before we more to action (an Effect), and reap the consequences.

The Mosaic Law in which the *Law of Sin and Death* operates acts like a mirror; it cannot but show our condition when we peer into it. A mirror doesn't have the power to clean our dirty face or brush our teeth--and neither does the Mosaic Law have the power to clean us up or make any changes in our lifestyle..

It was Christ who walked with Adam and Eve in the Garden of Eden. It was Christ who cast them out: Man's Destiny begins and end in Christ!

# CHAPTER FOUR
## THE DESTINY OF MAN

Samuel 10:1,6
1 "Then Samuel took a vial of oil, and poured it upon his head, and kissed him, and said, Is it not because the Lord has Anointed you Captain (King) over His inheritance? 6 And the Spirit of the Lord will come upon you, and you shall Prophesy with them [the other prophets], and shall be *turned into another man*."

*The Destiny of Man is about CHANGE, turned into another Man*. Our heavenly Father has gone to great extent to redeem His Human Creation. He planned before the foundation of the world to reveal His unfathomable riches in Glory, Wisdom and Knowledge in the Person of Jesus Christ. Jesus revealed the Father to us. Jesus gave us an extraordinary insight into the patriarchal bond, God's Love for the people of His heritage.

As the Father gave King Saul a new heart, the Anointing of the Holy Spirit upon him, a right Spirit and attitude to lead His people, God wants to give us a heart transplant too.

"For God so loved the world, that He gave His only begotten Son, that whosoever Believes in Him should not perish, but have Everlasting Life" (John 3:16). This great Love is called Agape Love. It's God's Holy embrace, His arms around Man.

God gave Heaven's Best: His Son. He doesn't want anyone to perish. This inspired Paul to write, "[God is]...longsuffering to usward, not willing that any should perish, but that all should come to Repentance" (2 Peter 3:9).

We must worship the Father for His Patience with us. It's God who had been wronged. He had the Indictment and Arrest Warrants to snatch us out of this world; all the Power and Authority to Convict and Sentence us to Hell was in His hands--but He chose to remain Patient, true to His Salvation Plan, yet urged us to Repent.

But, of course, as Man---Genius of Species---we didn't repent, and so over the generations the wrath of God kindled until it was appointed to fall on us, Justice Due, on a particular day and hour of that day; but instead---like the Ram in the Bush in Abraham day, Jesus of Nazareth was present to receive the punishment.

The Apostle John confirmed the Father's Love by quoting Jesus: "For the Father Himself Love you, because you Love Me, and have believed that I came from God" (John 16:27).

We may find it difficult to think of God as being our Father. Perhaps our earthly father didn't impress us. Perhaps his love was less than genuine, and his goodness suspect, or he left before we got to know him, thus failing to protect and provide for our emotional or material needs; or we may have suffered during a divorce, even abuse from him--but God as revealed by Jesus Christ is loving and extremely concerned about our daily life. In fact He wants to be part of it.

Make no mistake--God doesn't want to micromanage our life but be of assistance. "God is Love" (1 John 4:16). Not God is Management or Micromanagement.

The Fatherhood of God graciously unfolds in the many parables that Jesus told. Jesus proclaimed the Love, will and our relationship with Him. Jesus gave us an insight into His Character and Personality whereby we can intimately know Him and call Him Abba, Father.

Jesus said, "For your Heavenly Father knows what things you have need of, before you ask Him" (Matthew 6:8). But God is only the Father of Christians, and Christians are those who are Born Again and indwelled by His Holy Spirit. God is Creator of the Heavens and Earth, but He extends Fatherhood only to His Christian family, His Spiritual Children.

We're begotten by the *Spirit of Adoption* into God's Family. Then who is the father of the rest of Mankind? Satan is the father of Non-Christians: "You are of your father the Devil"(John 8:44).

Since Adam, the Family of Man without Christ belongs to the Family of Satan.

As Christians we Pray and stand in Faith that our Father is already aware of our needs. The relationship we have with Him isn't like the relationship God has with the unsaved masses. We have a Personal Relationship with a Personal Savior. We don't Pray with vain repetitions trying to persuade God to see things our way--that's manipulation, the "let's make a deal" mentality.

Unlike the heathens, we aren't trying to be self-righteous but depend on the Grace, Mercy and Guidance of our Heavenly Father who loves us unquenchably.

As the birds don't worry about finances, housing, meals, romance or other needs, we trust in our Father. Apostle Paul wrote:"But my God shall supply all your need according to His riches in Glory by Christ Jesus" (Philippians 4:19).

God takes care of the birds; we're more valuable than they are. We're created in the image and likeness of God. Because He has begotten us as Spiritual Children, He's obligated to take care of us.

Christianity isn't a Religion: It's not Cold or Legalistic but the Truth and Love of God: ***It's the One and Only Spiritual Path to God***. Our God is Warm, Personal, Tender and Affectionate. He can be known and befriended. When we get to know God we will never be the same. *Change in our Destiny.*

Ancient Israel witnessed the judgment and righteous indignation side of God which hates Rebellion and Disobedience. They knew Him as a fierce God who demanded Obedience; and when He didn't receive it---fire rained down from the sky!

Well, God hasn't changed! God cannot change. Thankful for us, the New Testament Covenant is with Jesus Christ as our Personal Lord and Savior; Jesus deals directly with us.

Understand, the Ministry of Jehovah-Elohim and His dealings with Man started with the ***Dispensation of Innocence*** (Adam & Eve in the Garden of Eden), the ***Dispensation of Conscious***

(Adam and his Descendants), then came the **Dispensation of Law** (Moses/Old Testament Covenant, From Abraham too Jesus of Nazareth, the Messiah).

The Ministry of Jesus Christ, the Messiah encompasses the **Dispensation of Grace**, the New Testament Covenant, and will continue to the Second Advent of Jesus Christ.

Since there is a difference in the Ministry and Personality of Jehovah-Elohim and Jesus Christ, is why we haven't seen fire coming down from Heaven, and cities scorched in response the wickedness of the Nations.

But, as with Israel, when God's Authority was answered with Obedience, He performed miracles of Protection, Healings and rain and food. For the most part Israel was afraid of Jehovah-Elohim. They didn't know Him as a God of Love. So they pursued and loved themselves, wealth and false gods, and let the Prophets person-ally deal with God.

However, the Father isn't shut out of the Earth because His Son is Ministering as High Priest. As in the Old Testament, even today Jehovah-Elohim speaks. His voice is distinct from that of the Son or the Holy Spirit.

The Elohim Unity, called the Trinity represents as three Persons. The Father's voice is the most dramatic and is seldom heard by mortal ears. "And the people saw the thundering, and the lightning, and the noise of the trumpet, and the mountain smoking: and when the people saw it, they removed and stood afar off. And they said unto Moses, Speak with us, and we will hear: but let not God speak with us, lest we die" (Exodus 20:18,19).

Paul wrote: "And the sound of a trumpet, and the *voice of words*, which voice they that heard entreated that the Word should not be spoken to them any more" (Hebrews 12:19).

The Father expresses Himself with brilliant effects. He comes forth with boldness and majestic oratory might that frightens the wits out of Human Beings. His looks are said to be beyond the Human mentality to accept. "And He said, You cannot see My face: For there shall no man see Me and live" (Exodus 34:20).

Therefore the Son and Holy Spirit are usually the two who communicate with Man.

The Lord Christ appeared many times in the Old Testament, New Testament and modern times as the representative of the Trinity. It's the Son and Holy Spirit who performs the Father's commands.

"Hear attentively the *thunder of his voice*" (Job 37:2). "And suddenly a *voice* came from Heaven, saying, "This is My beloved Son, in whom I am well pleased" (Matthew 3:17). John wrote, "Then a *voice* came from Heaven, saying, "I have glorified it and will glorify it again. The people therefore, that stood by, and heard it, said that it *thundered*; others said, An Angel spoke to Him. Jesus answered and said, This *voice* came not because of Me, but for your sakes" (John 12:28-30).

Another time the Father spoke directly from Heaven and produced an awe-inspiring reaction: "This is My beloved Son, in whom I am well pleased. Hear Him. And when the disciples heard it, they fell on their faces and were sore afraid" (Matthew 17:5, 6). Now the Father has committed everything to the Son.

We discover another reason why God became Man: it was to minister to us at our acceptance level. His humble, Human appearance made it comfortable for His disciples to learn.

Jesus said, "I and My Father are One" (John 10:30). It's God's desire that we share this unity (John 17:21, 23). He wants everyone to accept the words and deeds of Jesus Christ.

The Father desires that we Worship Him in the Person and the Name of Jesus Christ. God has conferred upon Jesus the Name that is above every name; that if we abide *In Him* and ask for anything in that Name we shall receive. All our needs are met through the interaction of the Trinity.

Jesus confirmed it by saying, "...if a man love Me, he will keep My words: And My Father will love him, and We will come unto him, and make Our abode with him" (John 14:23). We can take that promise to the bank!

We can relax in knowing that our every need will be met. We

have Faith and trust in the infallible Word of God. Confidently, we lay our burdens at the foot of His (and our) Cross; for He has said that he will never leave us nor forsake us.

Believing in His Word enables us to relax, not let worries and anxieties overwhelm us. We pray with definite requests---accurate Prayer and make our petitions known to Him. This is how we communicate with our Father, in Jesus' Name, the Architect of our Destiny. It's through the Son via the Holy Spirit (the Holy Spirit is the Spirit of the Father and the Spirit of the Son). He cares for us affectionately and watchfully.

> Matthew 11:28-30 (KJV)
> 28 "Come unto Me all you that labor and are heavy laden, and I will give you rest. 29 *take My yoke upon you*, and *learn of Me;* for I Am meek and lowly in heart; and you shall find *Rest* unto your souls. 30 For My yoke is easy, and My burden is light."

Compassion flowed from Jesus as He declared His undying Love for the multitude of people who pressed Him to hear the Word of God. He came into Creation to do the Father's Will. That Will was to change the lives of as many as would receive Him; His assignment was to turn the world upside down, rattle the cages of religion, shake the dungeon of Sheol, and break the rusty chains, the yoke of bondage off Man's precious neck.

From the Holy Scriptures we're certain that the virgin birth changed the lives of Joseph and Mary in a natural and profound spiritual way. She and Joseph were amazed that God used them; Mary conceive by the aid of the Holy Spirit; and Joseph rejoiced to be a part of God's Salvation Plan; Joseph loved, protected and provide for The Christ Child's emotional, physical and material needs.

During the years Jesus was in the home we can believe He prayed and the house was filled with the Glory Cloud, the Holy Spirit descended. Though He wasn't yet Baptized in the Spirit, He was a Believer in the greatest sense of the term. Jesus' mere Presence in the house brought blessings and the favor of God; it was like having the Ark of the Covenant in the house (2 Samuel 6:11). Mary and Joseph enjoyed great peace in knowing who He was--0 tidings of comfort and joy!

Jesus saw the multitude as lost sheep without a Shepherd. He taught them parables, compared the Kingdom of God with common things and life experiences to explain the Mysteries of God. He brought Grace and Truth to a spiritually bankrupt nation. He brought hope and love as a mighty river in a dry and thirsty land. He also taught them Discipline, Morals and Patience for the Kingdom of Heaven was at hand.

Satan had completely taken over Israel. He used Cesar the Emperor of Roman to humiliate and persecute the people. A dark cloud of doom loomed over the entire nation; demonic oppresssion of religions, cults, spiritual blindness, sicknesses, jealousy, envy, murder, political unrest, the foul fruit of Rebellion overcame Humanity.

The Judaism was powerless to break Satan's yoke of bondage, because the Sanhedrin Council added weight to the yoke.

Jesus taught that God loved them and desired their Obedience to His Son. That the Father was deeply moved to help them. He told them of the Father's Forgiveness and Grace. In accepting His words their lives miraculously changed as they cleaved to the gracious words that fell from His lips.

He taught them the Beatitudes; they were blessed to hear His Word, that Faith in the Word of God would conquer the Evil One and drive him from the Holy Lands.

Jesus proclaimed "the Spirit of the Lord is upon Me, because He has Anointed Me to preach the Gospel to the poor; He has sent Me to heal the brokenhearted, to preach Deliverance to the Captives, and recovering of sight to the blind, to set at liberty them that are bruised, to preach the *Acceptable Year of the Lord"* (Luke 4:18,19).

He was Man Anointed by the Holy Spirit to Preach, Heal and

Deliver the Captives. Believers *In Him* would receive blessings heaped upon blessings, pressed down, shaken together and overflowing in abundance; and their yoke would be destroyed because of the Anointing.

Jesus spoke of a great Rest for the Soul. This Rest was a portion of their Inheritance. As Children of Abraham they were entitled to the provisions of the Covenant including the Word of God, Healing and Deliverance from the torments and molestations of Unclean Spirits. "And they were astonished at His Doctrine: For HIS WORD WAS WITH POWER" (Luke 4:32).

"And in the synagogue there was a man, which had a Spirit of an Unclean Devil, and cried out with a loud voice...And Jesus rebuked him saying, Hold your peace, and come out of him.

And when the devil had thrown him in the midst, he came out of him, and hurt him not. And they were all amazed, and spoke am-ong themselves, WHAT A WORD IS THIS! (Luke 4:33, 35,36).

Jesus proved to the people that He was Anointed with the Holy Spirit. He demonstrated His Authority over Satan and his legions of demons. Jesus freed the Believers from their bondage. This undoubtedly changed their lives forever.

But the Religious Leaders challenged His claims and Authority. They looked down their noses at Jesus and questioned why He was always associating with sinners. "And Jesus answering said unto them, They that are whole need not a physician; but they that are sick. I came not to call the Righteous, but Sinners to Repentance" (Luke 5:26).

For the moment, the Council was satisfied with that answer; because in their eyes, those people around Jesus were the worst of sinners, but they, the Sanhedrin, were pure and righteous!

Yet Jesus of Nazareth wasn't welcome there; Members of the Sanhedrin Council, the Jewish Supreme Court heckled Jesus and sought to find an accusation against Him. Jesus healed the sick and the religious folks were insanely envious.

> Luke 7:12,14,15 (KJV)
> 12 "Now when He came nigh to the gate of the city, behold, there was a dead man carried out, the only son of his mother and she was a widow...14 And He came and touched the bier; and they that bare him stood still. And He said, young man, I say unto you, Arise. 15 And he that was dead sat up, and began to speak..."

Jesus by example demonstrated the Fatherhood of God by His personal lifestyle and actions. He loved people; there were no strangers. Jesus felt her emotions. He shed tears as He felt the depths of her loss; the despair, emptiness, a dark place in her Soul where the warmth of her son used to dwell.

Jesus had compassion on the poor, sick and those beaten down by circumstances. He hated Sickness and Death; His righteous anger lashed out at Demons including Sickness and Disease to destroy them; and the Demons ran at the hearing of His Word. They knew He was God in the Flesh, and on a mission to destroy the works of the Devil.

Jesus demonstrated the Will of the Father; it was the Father's Will and good pleasure that Jesus heal the sick and raise the dead. As He raised up the Physically Dead and they spoke again, so would He raise up the Spiritually Dead and they would speak with new Tongues. *He was Christ: The Resurrection and the Life*.

For three years Jesus walked the dusty trails preaching the Kingdom of God. At times He slipped away from the masses to rest, Pray and commune with the Father. The crowds were awesome, lost Souls pressing into the Kingdom.

"When the Evening was come, they brought unto Him many that were possessed with devils; and He cast out the spirits with His Word, and Healed all that were sick: That it might be fulfilled which was spoken by Isaiah the Prophet, saying, *Himself took our Infirmities and bare our Sicknesses*" (Matthew 8:16,17).

"And when He had called unto Him His Twelve Disciples, He gave them power against Unclean Spirits, to cast them out, and to Heal all manner of Sickness and all manner of Disease" (Matthew 10:1). Jesus appointed Twelve Disciples to delegate His Authority to.

Jesus chose ordinary men with little formal education. He didn't chose them as a new choice, neither for who they were in society, these men were *Predestined* according to the *Election of Grace*. The Father told Jesus who to choose: Twelve Disciples were Elected for this assignment before the world began.

Even Judas Iscariot who betrayed Jesus was foreordained for such a task. The Father knew Judas was a thief and a greedy man; that his greed would be exploited by Satan to betray Jesus.

The Father instructed Jesus to pick Judas thus allowing the betrayal to happen as God saw it through His Omniscience.

Jesus instructed the Twelve Disciples on how to exercise Authority over Satan. He taught them so they could one day teach others the **Destiny and Authority of the Man In Christ**.

"Verily I say unto you, whatsoever you shall *Bind on Earth* shall be *Bound in Heaven*; and whatsoever you shall *Loose on Earth* shall be *Loosed in Heaven*. Again I say unto you, that if two of you shall *Agree on Earth* as touching anything that they shall ask, it shall be done for them of My Father which is in Heaven. For *where two or three are gathered in My Name, there am I in the midst of them*" (Matthew 18:18-20).

And He told them to tell the world that the miracles He performed were rooted in Genuine Faith: "And these signs shall follow them that believe, in My Name shall they cast out Devils; they shall *Speak with New Tongues*" (Mark 16:17).

"And I heard the voice of the Lord saying, Whom shall I send and who will go for *Us?* Then said I, Here am I; send me" (Isaiah 6:8). Isaiah answered the call for someone to go forth in the Name of the Lord.

Now the Lord Jesus Christ is looking for Disciples---those alReady handpicked by the Father---to Anoint and send forth.

The work of God involves supernatural power. As Man we're compatible to receive the Holy Spirit. Now is the Apostolic Age. We must believe the Word of God and walk in the newness of life. Everything Jesus said is true and we can do all the things. But first we must believe...

The yokes imposed by Satan must be removed. Satan weighs us down with sins and useless baggage. He restricts our movement in time and space; he hinders our Prayers in the Heavens, and binds us through the Law of Sin and Death. He brings temptations and saturates our thought stream with filthy images, thoughts and delusions designed to water the poisonous tree within us.

He moves to oppress, obsess and possess our Soul to do evil. He schemes to infiltrate our soul wherein resides our psychic life powers and from there control our lives. His strategy is to shipwreck us with neurotic and psychotic behavior; emotional images and pseudo perceptions, violence, jealousy, perversion, worthlessness, hopelessness and suicide.

He leads us to believe we are nothing in God's eyes, and there's no help coming from beyond. Satan tries to destroy our confidence and use our bodies as waste containers to store his seeds of Iniquity, to be trafficked into our children and the world. Satan wants to forever hold onto our Inheritance!

However, God sent Jesus Christ to Anoint us, to pour the oil of the Holy Spirit upon our head. "And it shall come to pass in that day that his (Satan's) burden shall be taken away off our shoulder, and his yoke from off our neck, and **the yoke shall be destroyed because of the anointing**" (Isaiah 10:27).

The yoke of Satanic Oppression, the bondage of Sin and *Spiritual Death* is broken because of Jesus Christ, the Anointed One and His Anointing. That burden-bearing yoke-destroying power has arrived.

Now "When the enemy shall come in, like a flood; the Spirit of the Lord shall *lift up a standard against him*" (Isaiah 59:19).

The "flood" is not the enemy coming in, but the Holy Spirit. This is because the enemy sneaks in whereas the Holy Spirit has power, boldness, Authority, *Living Water* rushes in like the Congo River in the Rainy Season.

The ancient manuscripts doesn't have Punctuation or Chapters. So "When the enemy shall come in---like a flood the Spirit of the Lord will lift up a Standard against him."

The "Standard" is the Word of God that operates through the *Law of the Spirit of Life*. The Anointing is the Holy Spirit sent forth to empower us to be authentic Children of God. It's the Anointing--Christ Power that destroys the yokes of Sin, Sicknesses, Diseases and Poverty.

The Anointing also brings unity--that in itself is a change, because un-regenerated Man spurns the spiritual unity that Jesus Christ and the Father enjoys; but the regenerated Man enjoys the unity and commonalty with the Holy Trinity.

Jesus told the Disciples He had to leave and go back to the Father. He also told them He wouldn't leave them comfortless--for He promised them *never* to leave or forsake them.

Then He explained how He would leave and the Third Member of the Trinity would continue His work. "...it is expedient for you that I go away: For if I go not away, the Comforter will not come unto you; but if I depart, I will send Him unto you" (John 16:7).

When Jesus told them He was leaving, sorry filled their hearts. But He stressed that it was expedient: It was profitable and advantageous for them that He return to the Father and lay claim to the Name that is above all other names. He conferred the Authority of the Name upon the Church.

The Comforter (Counselor, Helper, Advocate, Intercessor, Strengthener, Standby) Jesus sent back to be in close fellowship with us. The Holy Spirit continues the Ministry.

Jesus again made a promise to believers receiving the Holy Spirit: " But you shall receive power, after that the Holy Ghost is come upon you; and you shall be witnesses unto Me... (Acts 1:8). Jesus' Word is always true, never fails.

Acts 2:1

1 "And when the Day of Pentecost was fully come, they were all [one hundred and twenty persons including Mary, mother of Jesus] with one accord [unity] in one place."

Only God can effect an everlasting change in us. He does this primarily from the Human Spirit to the outer Physical Body. Any attempt to change ourselves or others would be superficial and destined to failure. If we could Save, change, and conform ourselves into the image of God we wouldn't need God, The Holy Spirit or the Messiah. However, the Spiritual Rebirth comes from Heaven and not from Michigan State University.

The Holy Bible is the ONLY authoritative Rule of Faith and Conduct. The written Word is God-breathed, Authored by the Holy Spirit; it's not the thoughts of men that can be performed by men without divine intervention. But it's the Ministry of the Holy Spirit to bring about a change after our Repentance and Confession of Faith in Jesus Christ is made.

It's the mission of the Holy Spirit to bring our lives, deeds, behaviors, thoughts and motives Biblically in line with God's Word. Thus, the Holy Spirit empowers us to live the Christian Lifestyle. Without Him there can be no "good" **Destiny for Man,** no victory over the Devil and Sin.

# CHAPTER FIVE
## A NEW SPECIES

The Bible reveals in the Book of Job an unusual statement of life: "For man is born for trouble as the sparks fly upward" (Job 5:7). This Scripture was written to clarify that we are born into a fallen world, a perilous habitat, yet we must somehow survive and emerge victorious; failure isn't an option we want to settle for.

Even in the Animal Kingdom we observe the struggle of beast against beast, and beast against environment--the survival of the fittest. Truly the environment is cursed--but Christians aren't.

In the Garden of Eden God cursed the Devil and the ground-- but not Adam and Eve (Genesis 3:14-17; (some woman consider their monthly ministration a curse but it really isn't. God spoke only of pain in childbirth.). This was because God planned to redeem Man. Anyway, we aren't beast of the field but Human Spirits whom Jesus Christ died for and Resurrected.

And so we should exercise control over the "beastly" thoughts, emotions and actions. If we can't exercise control over ourselves we must seek help from an external source. This help can't come from the secular field of sciences, because their expertise is limited to the Psyche and Physical Body, of which they have only begun to understand.

Not to mention that these experts" have mental issues of their own. The Analysis needs an Analysis to keep the former's head straight is like the blind leading the blind; this won't suffice to bring about any lasting change, and often makes the patient worst, depended and addicted to Prescription Drugs and support groups the remainder of their lives.

The Spiritual Deadness of the Human Spirit is out of bounds to modern scientific probing. Yet once regenerated the Human Spirit is the real person conscious in the Spirit Realm. Only the Holy Spirit can strengthen a Human Spirit. God is that Spirit having supernatural powers to Resurrect, Heal and Counsel.

When we were Non-Christians our Human Spirit was *Spiritually Dead*; it was *comatose*, in a dream state, *unresponsive*, *powerless*, having *neither awake or aware* of *identity purpose, goals*, neither consciousness towards God or its own *Soul* and *Mind*, also housed in the same Physical Body.

When we experienced the New Birth we received the Presence of the Holy Spirit within our Human Spirit making us new creations, a New Species or Life Form. (2 Corinthians 5:17).

The basic principles of Spiritual Life are written in the Holy Bible. In its pages are the words of the Living God. God's Word is immutable and His Standard is that of Perfection: "Be you therefore perfect, even as your Father which is in Heaven is perfect" (Matthew 5:46).

We might say, "Well that's easy for you to say Jesus--You're God! How am I going to live holy on this demon-infested rock?" The same Holy Spirit that helped Jesus of Nazareth to live holy on this planet will help us. God wouldn't command us to do something we couldn't. Anything He requests beyond our Human capability He will manifest it through us.

Whereas, in the Soul Consciousness it's impossible to live Holy; and if the Human Spirit is dead the "house" is dark, condemned and unoccupied. Our own efforts at Holiness, self-righteousness will fail. The greater spiritual realities, godly attributes cannot be willed into existence.

The same principle applies to Salvation: We cannot Save ourselves neither can another Human Being Save us. The sooner we come to that realization and repent of our sins (Acts 2:38) the sooner we'll be on our way. \

It's through Repentance and Faith in the Lord Jesus Christ that we receive the gift of the Holy Spirit.

God recreates and inhabits our recreated Human Spirit then external changes begin. Understanding the Plan of Salvation and cooperating with the Holy Spirit definitely speeds up the process. This is answering God's Authority with Obedience and Faith.

King David wrote in Psalm 103 to express God's great Love for us. This Psalm describes what God does for us and what He's really like: He *Forgives all our Iniquities* and *Heals all our Diseases.* He *Redeems our life from destruction* and *Crowns us with Loving- Kindness and Tender Mercies.* He *Satisfies us with good food*, so we can remain physically strong. He *exercises Righteousness and Judgment for the oppressed* and *rebukes Satan in our behalf.* He's *Gracious, Slow to Anger, and Plenteous in Mercy.* He *Forgives our Sins and honors His Covenant* with us.

> Romans 10:8 (Amp. Bible)
> 8 "But what does it say? The Word (God's message in Christ) is near you, on your lips and in your heart; that is, the Word (the message, the basis and object of Faith...)

Salvation proceeds from the Atonement Blood of Jesus Christ It's a gift of God's Love for Mankind. The prerequisites to Salvation are Repentance and Faith in the Lord Jesus Christ.

Repentance plus Faith equals Conversion. Repentance involves the entire Soul and its Mental Facilities: The Intellect, Emotions, Will, and Imagination (Creativity). It's with the WHOLE HEART that we Believe (the Human Spirit isn't involved in the decision because it's Spiritually Dead).

We must Believe God's Word is infallible: "Whereby are given unto us exceeding great and precious promises; that by these you might be partakers of the Divine Nature..." (2 Peter 1:4).

In Faith, we lay hold of the Promises of God. We cannot doubt His ability to change our character, for His "precious Promises" are administered by Jesus Christ. After the New Birth we "are complete In Him." (Colossians 2:10).

Repentance means to be ashamed enough of our Sins to turn from them. It's not "turning over a new leaf" or a New Year's Resolution that seldom anyone takes seriously. Repentance involves feeling grief, empathy, remorse or sorrow in connection with our past sinful behavior; it also centers on an admission of guilt and an apology directed toward God; then comes the acceptance of the Lordship of Jesus Christ as Head of our life.

Repentance is embracing His sacrifice for our sins and our willingness to let Him Adopt us as Spiritual Children. Through Repentance we remove the obstacle standing between us and God; Repentance not only involves forsaking sin but turning to God--to adhere to, trust in, and rely on the Lord Christ, who is the Creator and Center of all things.

Repentance, as mentioned earlier, is an apology directed toward God, an Agreement and Reconciliation by means of Confirming that His indictment charging us as sinners is accurate and true: "For all have sinned, and come short of the Glory of God" (Romans 3:23). We throw ourselves upon the Mercy of His Supreme Court. This admission of Guilt always results in Acquittal!

One of the functions of the Holy Spirit is Adoption of Spiritual Children into the Family of God. Another of His functions is to convince us of Sin, Righteousness and Judgment (John 16:8). He's the one who impresses upon our heart the utter necessity and urgency to escape Hell, to be Saved by the Lordship of Jesus Christ.

After we're Saved He's the one who Cleanses, Sanctifies and keeps the Soul-Life Powers (our character and personality) under the watchfulness of the Law of the Spirit of life (1 John 1:9). The Holy Spirit makes living Holy and Sanctified obtainable.

"And the Spirit of God moved upon the face of the waters" (Genesis 1:2). In Creation the Holy Spirit is immediately recognized as the Spirit-power used by the Trinity to create. In this *Dispensation of Grace*, God the Father and God the Son aren't resident on earth but are both in Heaven. God the Holy Spirit is working in Creation.

The Father did His work through the Son who was Resurrected, and now seated at the Right Hand of God. When Jesus left, the Holy Spirit arrived on the Day of Pentecost to continue the ministry. Remember, the Holy Spirit is the Spirit of the Father and the Spirit of the Son. We can't communicate with the Father or the Son without the Holy Spirit to make the connection; and because the Son is the Messiah, the Savior of Man, we can't communicate with the Father except through the Son (John 14:6). "For through Him (Jesus Christ) we both have access by ONE SPIRIT unto the Father...in whom ye also are built together for an Habitation of GOD through the Spirit" (Ephesians 2:12,22).

So the Holy Spirit is the Spiritual Link between the Trinity; and He's our connection through His Presence within, making us a "habitation of God", a Oneness with the resident Holy Spirit in our recreated Human Spirit, and the unity of the Heavenly Church at the Throne of God. With this responsibility the Holy Spirit became the one who *Fellowships* with us.

Apostle Paul wrote to emphasize the Trinity and the Fellowship: "The Grace of the Lord Jesus Christ, and the Love of God, and the **Communion of the Holy Spirit** be with you all" (2 Corinthian 13:14). It's this "Communion" of the Holy Spirit we must have because He's the One who effects the Change, the Christlikeness we seek. As Jesus' Name is Wonderful, the Holy Spirit shares that Wonderful Name.

Fellowship implies dialogue: Because the Holy Spirit is a Person He has a distinct *personality*. He will speak within our recreated Human Spirit. He can also speak and be heard with our external ears; but as a Physical Person, like an Angel, He can appear to us in any form He wishes---but He doesn't have a permanent body. Jesus Christ has the only permanent (Glorified) Body of the Trinity for us to see with the physical eyes. Jesus is the only One of the Trinity who became a Legal Resident in Creation, was born into this world through a Human Female.

The Holy Spirit helps us to Pray to the Father in the Name of Jesus Christ. If it weren't for His promptings, we wouldn't feel the need to Commune, pray for lost Souls, the Sick and afficted; and our Prayer Life would be shallow and selfish.

In Prayer the Holy Spirit becomes our Spokesperson: "Likewise the [Holy[ Spirit also helps in our weaknesses. For we do not know what we should Pray for as we ought; but the [Holy]

Spirit Himself makes Intercession for us with Groanings [Unknown Tongue Prayer Language] which cannot be uttered. Now He who searches the hearts knows what the mind of the [Holy] Spirit is, because He makes intercessions for the Saints according to the Will of God" (Romans 8:26, 27).

Here's a Mystery: It's interesting to note the Holy Spirit helps us to Pray according to the Will of God---even using expressions "groaning" from His Heavenly Language. The Holy Spirit is Resident within our Human Spirit, and He's basically God; now, if God is in us and telling us what to Pray for and how to pray---*how can we fail to get what we ask for, since it's God using us, our lips, to pray to God?*

Truly, the Holy Spirit knows what our needs are, what we think we need, and what our Predestinated Service is, plus what Spiritual Gifts, Talents or Skills are needed to accomplish it. He will help us to Pray and manifest God's Perfect Will into our life. The Assignments has already been given out; it requires our Agreement in Prayer to manifest the Will of God on Earth as it is in Heaven.

Jesus said, "When the Helper comes, whom I will send to you from the Father, the Spirit of Truth who proceeds from the Father, He will *Testify of Me*" (John 15:26). The Holy Spirit will testify and Glorify Jesus Christ. It's His function to lead us to truth and reveal the Love of Christ. "For the love of God has been poured out in our hearts by the Holy Spirit who is given to us" (Romans 5:5). We must recognize His importance.

The Holy Spirit isn't an Archangel like Gabriel but God Himself. Apostle Paul described Him as follows: "Now we have received, not the spirit of the world, but the [Holy] Spirit who is from God, that we might know the things that have been freely given to us by God, These things we also speak, not in words which man's wisdom teaches but which the *Holy Ghost Teaches, comparing Spiritual Things with Spiritual*" (1 Corinthians 2:12, 13).

An important reason why the Holy Spirit is our Teacher: No

one knows God and the Holy Life better than the Spirit who is the Life of God. The Holy Spirit is the Author of the Bible Scriptures. It was He who guided the thoughts of the estimated forty Souls who over centuries compiled the Sacred Writings. As Jesus was the Teacher when He ministered on Earth, now the Holy Spirit is the Teacher of Christianity. The more we submit to the Word of God the more the Teacher will reveal Himself.

Our personal relationship with the Holy Spirit is in proportion to our Obedience to the Word of God. It is written: "For as many as are led by the Spirit of God, these are sons of God" (Romans 8:14). Even God is led by His Spirit; if that's good enough for Him, shouldn't it be good enough for us?

As we come humbly and submissive to the Holy Spirit, He will reveal Himself. Then as we become acquainted to His voice and promptings our relationship with Him becomes deeper. When we'll listen and freely discuss any problem in our lives, we'll experience Spiritual Growth and Maturity.

Christians need Biblical Principles and Power to live the Sanctified Life, and the Holy Spirit provides them. We're not to conform to the world but be transformed by the renewing of our minds. The world system was designed to conform us to the status quo; but God plan through the Empowerment of the Holy Spirit to conform us into the image of His Son.

In a wood fire the sparks fly upward because of the searing heat of combustion. The explosive nature of this fallen world, like an uncontrolled forest fire, fierce flames fanned by the Santa Anna Winds --ignites and devours the property and lives of everything and everyone in its grasp. It's the nature of the powers of this world, the "Resident Evil Ruler" to corrupt.

Though God remains the first cause of Creation, since then many causes, the will of Man and Demon Spirits misdirected and delayed God's Original Plan for Man. The furnace of Tribulations has brought many Souls to their knees. The Holy Spirit was given to change that; He's able to make "all things" work to gether for our Good in different Environments.

The Holy Spirit always had an awesome responsibility. Even before Creation, He sustained the Life of the Trinity, the created beings, angels and the Heavens of Heavens where dwells the Ancient One who inhabits Eternity..

Then Jehovah-Elohim spoke the Creation Commandment; the Word (Christ) formed the lower Spiritual Realms, and the "uncreated" astronomical mass that would later become the Material Universe; then the Holy Spirit manifested the Material Universe; igniting a magnificent explosion that split the mass and created galaxies, stars and planets; then He set them in motion in Outer Space.

At the appointed time "...the Spirit of God moved upon the face of the water" (Genesis 1:2). And Earth became ready for Man, the *Genius of Species*.

"The Lord God formed Man out of the dust of the ground, and breathed into his nostrils the *Breath of Life*; and Man became a living Soul" (Genesis 2:7). When God breathed into Adam the "*Breath of Life*", He released the **Original Human Spirit made in God's image and likeness**; and when this Human Spirit interacted with his Physical Body it produced his Soul Body, in order to connect with the Physical Body, its Five Senses, and therefore be in contact with the Physical Universe.

The Soul Body was strategically positioned between the Spirit Body and the Physical Body. The Soul Body functions as a go-between: it receives and passes on information from the Human Spirit to be assimilated by the Soul-Mind, and when necessary the Mind can engage the Physical Body to initiate an action within the Physical World.

In the opposite direction, the Five Senses located in the Physical Body relay information to the Soul-Mind; its Mental Facilities Evaluates, Thinks and Reasons. Thus the Soul Body has the Mind Facilities of Intellect, Emotions, Will, and Imagination, to render decisions on the condition of the Physical Body and environment. The Soul keeps a Chronological Record, stores memories, information, and experiences as it sojourns in this lower Realm.

The Soul Body possesses our personality, and the "I" that makes us an individual. It's the individual "I" and God-given free Will that draws us into conflict with the Holy Spirit.

With the Five Physical Senses we contact the world around us; with these same Five Senses Satan contacts and influences us.

Sensory Perception on a Psyche, Soul-Life Level is subject to interference, distortions, deceptions and illusions. Knowing about the Mental-Psyche Nature of Man, Satan wars against our Soul and Physical Bodies. Satan knows that Man without the Holy Spirit is *Spiritually Dead* and can't receive help from there; so he mainly tries to keep us from hearing the Gospel of Jesus Christ and the beautiful Voice of the Holy Spirit.

The corrupted Mind can become a wasteland of Iniquity, a landfill of stinking, rotting garbage thoughts. Fortunate for us the Word of God enables us like the eagle to fly above the Psyche- Soul-Life Realm of ordinary thinking and living.

"For the Word that God speaks is alive and full of power [making it active, operative, energizing, and effective]; it is sharper than any two-edged sword, penetrating to the *dividing line of the Soul and [Human]Spirit,* and of joints and marrow [of the deepest parts of nature], exposing and sifting and analyzing and judging the very thoughts and purposes of the heart" (Hebrews 4:12).

When we were un-regenerated, Non-Christians our shriveled up, depleted Human Spirit and Soul were united into one carnal, highly functional, intelligent nature.

As stated earlier, our Human Spirit was senseless and indifferent towards God, its own existence, identity, divinity, purpose, and was powerless to perceive or participate in the Spiritual or Material World.

That's why the Crucifixion of Jesus of Nazareth and Pentecost changed everything. The Balance of Power shifted from the Kingdom of Darkness to the Kingdom of Light. We were slaves to Sin and it's ugly Trafficker; we had Iniquity planted in us and we loved to Sin; a Psychic yoke upon our necks. But when we believed the Word of God we were transformed, Sealed with God's kiss, and Separated by the Word, the dividing action of the Holy Spirit; our recreated Human Spirit was separated from our Soul and also positioned *In Christ*, at the Throne *With Christ*.

> Ephesians 1:13 (Amp. Bible)
> 13 "In Him you also who have heard the Word of Truth, the glad tidings (Gospel) of your Salvation, and have believed in and adhered to and relied on Him, were *Stamped with the Seal* of the long-promised Holy Spirit."

We were not so fortunate to be "born" like Adam who stood up (perhaps a teenager) filled with the Presence of God. Yet, now we still can be New Creatures in Christ through the Spirit of Truth, the Spirit of Adoption (Romans 8:15).

Job said, "The Spirit of God hath made me, and the *Breath* of the almighty gives me life" (Job 33:4). The Breath of Life is another name for the Holy Spirit.

The same Holy Spirit encourages us to "Be filled with the Spirit, speaking to one another in Psalms and Spiritual Songs, singing and making melody in your heart to the Lord" (Ephesians 5:16,19).

We must say to Him, "Holy Spirit breathe on me! Cause me to know the exceeding riches that are available to me in Christ Jesus. Change me daily into the image of Jesus Christ; call me by Your Grace and use me in Your Ministry."

As Jesus of Nazareth offered Himself to God through the eternal Spirit (Hebrews 9:14), so we offer ourselves; Spirit, Soul and Body through the same Spirit to be presented Holy like Him.

For the **Holy Spirit is also Lord**; yet at the same time He was not sent to exalt Himself but to exalt the Lord Jesus Christ: "***now the Lord is that Spirit; and where the Spirit of the Lord is, there is liberty***" (2 Corinthian 3:17). The Holy Spirit is equal to the Lord Jesus Christ, because He is the Spirit of the Lord Jesus

Christ. It's our responsibility to learn from Him, be led into the truth. He will separate for us Spiritual Things from worldly things and encourage us to seek after the things of God.

"But we all, with unveiled face, beholding as in a mirror the Glory of the Lord, are transformed into the same image from glory to glory, just as by the *Spirit of the Lord*" (2 Corinthian 3:17,18). Therefore, understand that "It is god which works in you both to will and to do His good pleasure" (Philippians 2:13).

With our face veiled, we can't see where we are going or where we have been. When we were in Darkness, how gloomy it was! As long as we are kept blind and dumb, Satan will forever lord it over us. But now the Light of God has come, and our eyes are opened wide; we see with an unveiled face the One who Loves us and sent His Son to die for us.

As Redeemed Children of God, we look in the mirror and the Spirit of Life changes us--- not like those who look into the mirror and the Law of Sin and Death convicts but doesn't change anything--- we see ourselves and the Glory of the Lord. It is the work of the Spirit of the Lord.

In the Old Testament, the Holy of Holies was hidden from Man behind a thick curtain called the Veil. Only the High Priest was allowed to enter, once a year, to offer animal blood. Now, through Jesus Christ, the Veil has been ripped, made obsolete and done away with entirely. We who were far off and strangers to God and the Promise have been brought near by the Blood of Jesus Christ, the Messiah and High Priest of the Heavenly Sanctuary.

These Scriptures should put our Soul at ease knowing the Holy Spirit is God. Christ in us is God, and He's working to bring keep us on the path of our Appointed Destiny.

# CHAPTER SIX
## THE RESIDENT EVIL

The Wisdom and Knowledge of God and Creation is written in the Holy Bible. The Bible expresses the "Omniscience" of God (to use the words "thoughts" or "mind" is inaccurate when describing God's Knowingness); in the Bible are His Plans, Purposes and Pursuits. The Bible also expounds upon the plans, purposes and pursuits of His Archenemy: Satan (No last name)

In order for us to understand the struggles on the road to *Destiny*, we must know all we can about the Major Players.

The Holy Spirit compelled the writers of the Bible to write many profound truths into the depths of its pages, causing the interpretations not to be as obvious as the general framework; and because of the complexity of the plans of God, there are different levels of consciousness the writers experienced and struggled to put into meaningful words.

On the surface the Bible may appear to refer to a mortal person or nation. As our Spiritual Eyes are open by the Holy Spirit we discover the Scriptures have duel meaning, often referring to something entirely different; it's only Truth understood at a higher level of consciousness.

> Ezekiel 28:14,15
> 14 "You are the Anointed Cherub that Covers: and I have set you so; you were upon the Holy Mountain of God; 15 You were *perfect* in your ways from the day you were created. Until *Iniquity* was found in you."

The Prophet Ezekiel was the instrument the Holy Spirit used to explain to us the origin of Satan, the Resident Evil. He was also known as Lucifer whose name means Light Bearer. He was the Anointed Cherub (v.14) who stood directly before God. He guarded the entrance to the lofty place of the Ancient One, the Almighty God. Lucifer was said to be gorgeous, the most beautiful creature in Heaven. He radiated light and heavenly music gravitated in percussion waves from his person (v.13). It's widely believed that he was the Minister of Heavenly Music.

But his heart smote him and he became lifted up with pride, vain because of his beauty and importance. According to the Scriptures: "You have defiled your sanctuaries by the multitude of your Iniquities; by the *Iniquity of your Traffic*" (v.18). The Archangel Lucifer trafficked Iniquity by persuading on third of the angels to rebel and Sin against God.

> Isaiah 14:12-14)
> 12 "How are you fallen from Heaven, 0 Lucifer, Son of the Morning! How are you cut down to the ground, which did weaken the nations! 13 For you have said in your heart, I WILL ascend into Heaven, I WILL exalt my throne above the stars of God; I WILL sit also upon the Mount of the Congregation... 14 I WILL ascend above the heights of the clouds: I WILL be like the Most High [God]."

The Prophet Isaiah received by the Holy Spirit another piece of the cosmic puzzle. "How are you fallen from Heaven, 0 Lucifer..." became a haunting melody of Grace, betrayal and Expulsion."I will ascend...I will exalt...I will sit...I will be..." were his words of Rebellion; I WILL and not THY WILL sealed his fate.

Out of his mouth came the confession of his heart. It was no longer God's Will that concerned him but his own will. He believed in his heart he was more worthy to be praised than God. So it was no longer acceptable for him to bow to God.

He coveted the adoration of the heavenly host, one-third of the multitude of Angelic Beings. When God rebuked his rebellious heart he declared an open season on every spirit loyal to God.

Revelations 12:7,9,12 (KJV)

7 "There was a war in Heaven: Michael and his angels fought against the Dragon; and the Dragon fought and his angels, 9 And the Great Dragon was cast out, that old serpent called the Devil, and Satan, which deceives the whole world; he was cast out into the Earth, and his angels ... with him. 12 ...Woe to the inhabitants of the earth and the sea! For the Devil is come down unto you having great wrath, because he knows that *he has but a short time."*

The Apostle John added another piece to the puzzle. He received by the Holy Spirit Revelation Knowledge about the war that took place in Heaven. Lucifer, now Satan (the Accuser) fought against the Archangel Michael and his two-thirds of the multitude of angels loyal to the Ancient One (It's commonly believed that Lucifer once had authority over the Archangels Michael and Gabriel.)

In the war against God, Satan couldn't use the delegated Anointing of the Holy Spirit against God (God's Holy Spirit will NEVER turn on Him); Satan used a *power* generated by his rebellious attitude, a *power* that never existed in Heaven until Satan created it; a power that influenced angels.

With this power and Free Will to use it, Satan blasphemed, manipulated, hindered and interrupted the peace and order of Heaven; he initiated Rebellion, Intimidation, Domination and Violence among the governing ranks of angels.

But Satan was defeated, "cast down to the earth" and his angels with him. They were stripped of their former duties and powers; and since they were created beings with a will, they were cursed to forever remain in their fallen state (there was no Redemption, Salvation Plan for the angels that sinned).

These fallen angels became known as Evil Spirits, Demons, Devils, and Unclean Spirits. (But since Adam, the expelled Ruling Angels from Heaven now reign on Earth as Principalities,

Powers, Rulers of the Darkness, Prince Spirits, and Territorial Spirits in the Atmospheric Heaven around the world.)

The former segment of Scripture comes with a Warning: "Woe!" We as inhabitants of the Earth are now the targets of Satan's wrath. Not only is he angry at God but all of God's Creation. He is especially violent towards Christians because we made it out of his dungeon.

Satan is depraved and reprobate. His army of evil spirits could well number in the millions. Satan is knowledgeable of our Human soul-psyche nature. He has the knowledge to manipulate and operate through the *Law of Sin and Death*, to bind people unaware of his or the existence of this Law, and those who willfully sin.

He has the knowledge of the Word of God though he doesn't trust in or rely upon it--but manipulates it to suit his evil purpose; he has the ability to manipulate the Laws of Nature to produce magic, illusions, visual and sound effects, mental deceptions and psychic phenomena; he has knowledge of our Human Anatomy and sends spirits of sicknesses and diseases to cripple or destroy our body; he's aware of our weaknesses, our mental and physical needs; he uses the knowledge to snare us.

He has many things in his favor but he doesn't have the yoke-destroying power of the Holy Spirit! Neither is he Omnipresent, Omnipotent and Omniscient like our God!

He can't acquire, manipulate or appropriate the Holy Spirit to assist him in any way. But we are indwelled and filled with the Holy Spirit to assist us to resist Satan's schemes, dwarf his plans to *Traffic Iniquity* and calamity.

Satan remembers who he was before Creation. Because he was so close to God he knows things that the other angels don't know. This gives him advantage over them to bind and hinder their work in Creation. But unlike God, Satan isn't Omnipresent, Omnipotent, and Omniscient. Satan can only manipulate at will what's already created; he has no true Creative Powers; neither can he control us unless we submit and allow it----thus giving Human territory, the Self-Life over to him.

Therefore he acquires "control" primarily by deception, *bait and switch*. He presents something or someone on the surface seems good, then it or they turns evil and dangerous.

The Apostle Peter wrote: "For if God spared not the angels that sinned, but cast them down to Hell, and delivered them into **Chains of Darkness**, to be reserved unto judgment" (2 Peter 2:4).

Reading this Scripture we can prematurely conclude that "all" the fallen angels are securely locked away in Hell. That is not the case; what the Scriptures state that the fallen angels are bound to the earth and beneath it, and cannot as a group ascend back into Heaven; otherwise, the Unclean Spirits Jesus cast out were a figment of His imagination; and Satan could not have corrupted Adam and Eve, incited David to number Israel or tempted Jesus of Nazareth in the desert---if Satan and his legion were already incarcerated in Hell. Yet it is likely Hell is well-staffed!

These fallen angels are thriving in and among Mankind. The Word says their time is running out: There are so many people to kill and so little time; so they have stepped up their campaign.

It's commonly believed that Adam and Eve knew about the rebellion of Lucifer. There's references to Lucifer being present at some time in the Garden of Eden: "You has been in Eden the Garden of God" (Ezekiel 28:13).

The Anointed Cherub returned to Eden the last time as Satan, and stole the Throne of the Earth and the lower heavens.

Adam knew the nature of God was represented in the Tree of Life and the nature of Satan in the Tree of Knowledge of Good and Evil. Since God told Adam about the two Trees it's logical that he knew what they represented; and when God gave Adam Dominion, God-of-this-Realm Status, He explained to him that the Adversary of his Eden Kingdom was Satan.

God's enemy was Satan; therefore Adam's enemy was Satan. The Bent One stalked Eve and planned his strategy. The attack came swiftly: "And he said unto the woman, "Yea, has God said, You shall not eat of every tree of the Garden? (Genesis 3:1). Satan sparked Eve's curiosity. What he said was "Could it be that God has said?" He introduced doubt into her consciousness--a question concerning the Word of God which she had never beforehand questioned. He introduced the temptation for her to consider another course of action; instead of blind Obedience and Faith, she could exercise her *individuality*, her *Free Will*, and her self-motivated independence.

Satan insinuated God was withholding something from her. He implied that God was unfair in His relationship with her, His Goodness was Self-Seeking; God was selfish and strict in sharing His Wisdom and Knowledge; and though Adam was content in blindly following God, she should be a *Liberated Woman* and follow her own mind regardless of what God or her husband did.

She agreed with Satan and accepted his line of reasoning. She unconsciously amended the Word of God that was in her heart. God said, "...you shall not eat of it [the fruit of the Tree of Knowledge]; for in the day that you eat thereof you shall surely die" (Genesis 2:17). But she said, "God has said, You shall not eat of it, *neither shall ye touch it*, lest you die" (Genesis 3:2).

She changed the words of God and substituted her own. Satan got Eve to accept her own words over God's Word, he had no difficulty getting Eve to accept his words over hers. He replied confidently, "You shall not surely die" (V.4). She immediately accepted his words as the Gospel Truth.

Temptation wasn't Sin, but yielding to the temptation, disobeying God amounted to Sin..

Both Adam and Eve were expelled from the Garden. Access to the Tree of Life was denied. If they'd eaten of it in their fallen state they would become immortal yet depraved creatures.

Their Rebellion brought Sin, and Sin brought *Spiritual Death*, Sickness and Calamity into their bodies and their descendants suffered from the cradle to the grave. Life was hard and with few rewards.

The battle lines between Good and Evil, the Children of God and those of Satan were established: Satan sent forth a Spirit of Jealousy and provoked Cain to murder his brother Abel (Genesis 4:8). Cain destroyed his brother because Abel's offering to God, the blood of the lamb was accepted and commended by God; and Cain's works were rejected as rebellious and evil.

Abel's Obedience and Righteousness by Faith enabled him to experience a personal relationship with God; he accomplished this by the blood atonement for his Sins. But Cain's offering, the fruit of the cursed ground wasn't accepted. It represented Satan, him reign over Man with an iron fist.

He targeted the descendants of Adam, specifically Abel, who would father the Hebrews and bring forth the Messiah.

Cain's offering also exposed the presence of a religious spirit-- righteousness by Human works alone. His foundation was based on Rebellion to the established Word of God.

Thereafter Cain went forth preaching religion, rituals and idol worship, a self-righteous gospel that *Trafficked Iniquity*, and caused false doctrines to gain momentum, to perversely affect the Souls of Man, to keep him bound by Invisible Chains of Darkness---like the fallen angels--- until death overtakes Man: Bound hand and foot from cradle to grave.

"And it came to pass, when men began to multiply on the face of the Earth...And God saw that the wickedness of Man was great in the earth, and that every imagination of the thoughts of his heart was only evil continuously. And it repented the Lord that He had made Man on the Earth, and it grieved Him to His heart" (Genesis 6:1, 5, 6).

Six Chapters into the Book of Genesis and God was ready to destroy His Creation called Man. The "Sons of God" being Abel's descendants intermarried with the "daughters of men" of Cain's descendants and an explosion of evil permeated civilization.

But Noah found Grace in the sight of God. After the Flood, a remnant of Man remained on the earth; but the past generations of Man were hidden away safely in Sheol until the Messiah, the

*Kinsmen Redeemer* would free them.

"And Satan stood up against Israel, and provoked David to number Israel" (1 Chronicles 21:1). This is the first time the name "Satan" was used in the Old Testament. Many times the term "Evil Spirit" was used to describe demonic spirit activity.

Israel was God's Elect, His Chosen People to bring forth the tabernacle of flesh that would cloth the Messiah. This was why he personally rose up against Israel:

David was a man after God's own heart. David knew who he was---the Anointed King of Israel. David also knew his Covenant Rights.

For centuries Satan's ground forces dug in and infiltrated into the Hebrew Nation and surrounding areas. His wicked influence lurked behind the mortal thrones of kings who ruled nations with a heavy, often murderous hand.

Armed with false religions, the idol worshipping and snake pits of Sin called "high places," orgies, prostitution, mutilations and Human sacrifices were offered to the gods--he slithered into the mainstream of every civilization. These distractions keep Man busy satisfying himself and indifferent towards Jehovah-Elohim, the One True God.

During the Holy Wars of the Lord, David experienced outrageous victories over the enemies of God. Because of this David wanted to boast about Israel's triumphant Army.

Satan took advantage of David's desire and personally incited David by the Spirit of Pride. David took a census of his military in direct violation of God's instruction; that not by power or might but by His Spirit Israel should trust. The Lord wanted Israel to depend on Him rather than their own strength or weapons.

Because of this transgression "God sent an angel unto Jerusalem to destroy it; and as he was destroying, the Lord beheld, and He repented [forgave] him [David] of the evil, and said to the angel that destroyed, It is enough, stay now your hand" (1 Chronicles 21:15). The same Destroyer Spirit that brought death to the first born in Egypt brought death to the Elect numbering seventy thousand men. Thus Satan incites Man and Man pays the price.

>Numbers 13:30,31 (KJV)
>30 "And Caleb stilled the people before Moses, and said, *Let us go at once, and possess it; for we are well able to overcome it.* 31 But the men that went up with him said, *we be not able to go up against the people; for they are stronger than we."*

The Wars of the Lord began hundreds of years before David was born. He inherited the mistakes that were made by Israel. In this section of scripture when Moses began the ground assault against the walled cities and nations within the Promised Land, Israel didn't face only a flesh and blood battle but a *Spiritual Warfare* against the evil creatures whispering in the ears of the kings.

The twin Spirits of Fear and Doubt oppressed them. On this first attempt the demonic forces deceived the ten scouts into believing they couldn't conquer the "superior" inhabitants. Israel saw the enemy as giants and themselves as grasshoppers; this was only in their "own" eyes. It was the slave mentality revisited upon them from Egypt; the Deceiver was again at work.

They experienced with their Five Senses the illusion Satan wanted them to see and believe. He inflicted them with Low Self-Esteem. Though Israel was the Elect, they considered themselves without God's arm, inferior, unworthy to possess the land; and they ultimately received what they believed.

Their shortcomings became their obsession instead of God their strength. They forgot the Lord was the strength of their lives, that Faith was believing what can't be seen but hoped for.

Israel should've trusted in the Lord God. The Greater One was with them but they failed to believe it, to reach out and touch Him. He would've delivered the fortified cities into their hands.

Joshua and Caleb declared "WE ARE WELL ABLE." They confessed with their mouths what they believed in their hearts:

God is able to keep His Promises! These men had Faith to believe: The bigger they were the harder they'd fall. Great is the army who carries God's Word.

The Congregation, being spooked couldn't enter into the rest, though it was promised and prepared for them before the foundation of the world.

"Son of man, say unto the Prince of Tyrus, Thus says the Lord God: Because your heart is lifted up, and you have said, I am God, I sit in the seat of God in the midst of the seas; yet you are a man, and not God...By your great wisdom and by your *traffic* have you increased your riches, and your heart is lifted up..." (Ezekiel 28:2,5).

Previously, Ezekiel prophesied against the City of Tyre. Now he focused on Tyre's leadership. A Spirit of Pride was upon this ruler. He thought he was God Himself. But the deeper interpretation of these verses concerned the "invisible" King of Tyre: Satan, whom the people were really following.

Hidden in the personality of the King of Tyre was the Spirit of Pride; above him were the invisible, powerful strings that made him dance like a marionette. Jehovah-Elohim compared him to the Anointed Cherub that Covers: Lucifer (V.4).

The King of Tyre was but a front, a doorway for spirits to go back and forth between realms; the seat where the Prince Spirits, Rulers of the Darkness expressed themselves to control the Physical Realm and civilizations.

At another time in the sojourn of Man, Daniel was God's chosen vessel: "Then said he unto me, Fear not, Daniel: For the first day that you set your heart to understand, and to chasten yourself before your God, your words were heard, and I am come for your words. But the *Prince of the Kingdom of Persia* withstood me one and twenty days [by Daniel's description, the angelic messenger appeared gloriously powerful; Daniel 10:5,6]; but Michael, one of the Chief Princes [Archangels], came to help me; and I remained there with the Kings of Persia" (v.12,13).

Daniel fasted and prayed to God for the release from captivity

God heard his prayer and immediately sent an angelic messenger to Daniel. But the Prince of Persia kidnapped the messenger? Not hardly--the mortal prince couldn't detain an angelic messenger; it was a Demonic Prince, a Territorial Ruler.

The angel said that the Archangel Michael freed him. The Archangel Michael is often mentioned as a warrior-class being loyal to God (Jude 1:9 Revelation 2:7-12). Michael was the angel who led the charge against Satan during the War in Heaven. At the end he will also chain Satan and throw him into the Pit.

The angel who talked with Daniel returned to fight against the Prince of Persia (the Demonic Ruler) but after the Prince of Persia, the Prince of Grecia would take its place. Both Princes worked for Satan; and what the angel told Daniel was prelude to the conquest of that nation.

This conquest depended on the present Demonic Prince of Persia being removed, whereas the Prince of Grecia would succeed him. When the demonic spirit operating behind the throne was succeed, then the mortal leadership on Earth would likely change accordingly; there's disorder, ambition, strife, jealousy and envy in the demonic ranks; they don't get along any more than the leaders of our society agree on how things should be done.

However, the angels loyal to God keep the pressure on these Demonic Rulers to relinquish their territories and strongholds. The fight over Human Souls continues...

History records that Babylon was defeated by the Medo-Persians. Persia was defeated by Greece (Grecia ); God's providence also plays an important part in what is allowed to take place on Earth.

> Matthew 2:1, 2 (KJV)
> 1 "Now when Jesus was born in Bethlehem of Judaea in the days of Herod the King, behold there came Wise Men from the East. 2 Saying, Where is He that is born King of the Jews? For we have seen His Star in the East, and are come to Worship Him."

Herod the Great was quite disturbed when the three Wise Men inquired about the King of the Jews. Herod wasn't the rightful heir to the throne of David. If the Messiah became the Heir, perhaps a riot would break out and Rome would replace Herod as King. Herod was already a paranoid ruler. He was suspicious of his own relatives; he also killed several of them.

Herod was advised by the Sanhedrin Council concerning the prophecies of the expected Messiah. Herod had Human advisers plus invisible throne-controlling Spirits who dominated Israel through their central stronghold deep within the Senate of the Roman Empire. From there they controlled the known world.

Herod the Great and the Sanhedrin Council were used by Satan to kill the Prince of Peace before he came into His Kingdom.

Herod and all Jerusalem were troubled. The Spirits that possessed Cain also possessed Herod and those loyal to his Regime. Herod ordered the murders of the two year old boys.

Satan waited thousands of years to prevent the Messiah from incarnating; he failed to stop the birth but he planned to leave no doubt of His fate.

Since the Garden of Eden, the terror of the "woman's Seed" crushing his head was a constant companion, a reminder of his imminent defeat; one day he would be forced off his throne--but until then he would fight!

Many times Satan tried to "ethnic cleanse", murder the Elect people (Exodus 1:16 Esther 3:9). But God spared a remnant.

Satan seduced Israel into immorality, idol worship, religions and following false prophets. Disobeying God became a religion of its own; it took on creative and exhaustive dimensions!

Now Satan was faced with his worst nightmare: The incarnation into the Physical Realm of the Word, Christ, Messiah. The One Jehovah-Elohim proclaimed and declared with an oath: The Center of Creation, Who formed the worlds---was coming to live on Earth as Man!

Matthew 4:3,10 (KJV)

3 "And when the Tempter came to Him, he said, If You be the Son of God, command these stones to be made bread. 10 Then said Jesus unto him, Get you hence, Satan: For it is written, You shall Worship the Lord your God, and Him only shall you serve."

The temptations of Jesus of Nazareth weren't different from the temptations that we face. Since the Fall of Adam and Eve, the Devil hasn't changed his strategy. For the most part why should he change when his system is so effective? However his strategy didn't work on Jesus.

Satan used the word "if" Jesus was the Son of God, urging Jesus to prove Himself. If Satan believed Jesus wasn't God's Son he wouldn't have tested Him; Satan knows everyone who belongs to him, and he knew Jesus wasn't a slave to Sin. His probing was designed to undermine, cause Jesus to doubt the outcome of this temptation.

He also wanted Jesus to question who He was, the Father's ability to protect and provide for Him while on earth, as being limited (by choice), subjected to the cloth of misery.

Satan also wanted the Savior to perform for vainglory, to make bread from stones and satisfy His hunger. The Enemy sought to exploit a natural Human need into a supernatural show.

Then the Devil "took Him" by magic and set Him on the highest point of the holy temple. There he tempted Jesus to jump, commit suicide under the pretence of misapplied Scripture; the same trick he played on Eve. Satan misquoted Psalms 91:11 "lest you dash your foot against a stone." He said, "lest at *anytime* you dash..."

Satan wanted Jesus to challenge God to keep His Word based on a distortion of the Word. His purpose was for *Jesus* to question whether God loved Him enough to "alter" His Word to protect Jesus from death. Insecurity was the emotional response Satan was after; God Word is forever fixed.

Satan offered Jesus the kingdoms of the world. Jesus didn't dispute that Satan owned them. He offered Jesus to give Him back the entire world in exchange for His Praise and Worship. Satan wanted Jesus to cash in on the jackpot, instant Glory, Power and Fame. Yet Jesus rebuked him like one would rebuke a foolish child!

"From that time Jesus began to preach, and to say, Repent: For the Kingdom of Heaven is at hand" (Matthew 4:17).

As Christians we must stand our ground and fervently pray that God's will be done on Earth as it is in Heaven. The reason why Heaven is a wonderful place is that God's Will is a continuous "yea", whereas on the earth its usually "nay".

We must learn to answer God's Authority with Obedience to the Word and continuously commune with His Holy Spirit. Our prayers are needed to edify Christians everywhere.

In the new millennium the world continues to be infested with fallen angels poised to pounce and dictate their wills into our lives. These spirits have existence but no meaningful lives. They infiltrate to experience our lives, take over our Soul and Physical Bodies, assimilate our Will, Intellect, Imagination and Emotions.

Emotions especially attract their attention. They want to feel, to experience the burning, Human sensuality and lust, the primitive drive, unrestrained passions, anger, hatred and violence. They maneuver, assimilate and change the social morality standards, corrupt the nation and make this Realm a living Hell.

These Messengers of Evil Calamity, thorns in our sides are veteran assassins following orders from a greater evil.

Concerning this Apostle Paul wrote to the Ephesians Church:

> Ephesians 6:12 (Amp. Bible)
> 12 For we are not wrestling with flesh and blood [contending only with physical opponents], but against the Despotism, against the Powers, against [the Master Spirits who are] the World Rulers of this present darkness, against the Spirit Forces of Wickedness in the heavenly (supernatural) spheres."

Apostle Paul wrote that the full armor of God is necessary to take a stand against the satanic opposition. We're to hold our ground--not advance or attack the enemy headquarters. Our weapons are: Truth, Righteousness, Gospel of Peace, Faith, Salvation, and the Sword of the Spirit which is the Word of God.

The enemy of our Spirit, Souls, and Physical Bodies will introduce through other people all sorts of arguments, theories, reasoning and mental gymnastics to keep us preoccupied, distracted from the real issue: Standing on the Word of God and tightly cleaving to His Christ.

Yet the Truth of the Word of God will destroy every yoke and bondage. Christians aren't immune to Satan's schemes. That's why we must be aware and monitor our thoughts to take captive evil thoughts that are contrary to the Word and Obedience of Christ. Let Him be Lord of our Dreams, Thoughts and entire life.

Civilization is in a state of decline. The Holy Bible reveals in its magnificent text how iniquity entered the world, entrenched and elbowed its way into our life; it's goal is to press us into the grave.

The Resident Evil, Satan and his demonic Legions came to steal, kill and destroy us. It should be obvious to anyone who has a functioning brain and lives in this hostile environment that something is seriously wrong with this world and those who live in it.

Many attempt to dispute or minimize the existence of God or Satan, but fail to explain why things aren't getting any better. Crime has skyrocketed, prisons are full, no peace on earth, starvation, civil wars and genocide; people are barbaric, selfish, materialistic and greedy as ever.

In America, the citizens look to the President of the United States to solve the problems with our society. Candidate promise all types of change, but in reality, nothing will change until the Prince and Territorial Spirits that rule over America are dealt with; and the President and Supreme Court are subject to these Evil Spirits (Non-Christian Public Office holders are particularly useful in the trafficking of Iniquity; Satan uses them to change moral laws---God's Moral Standards for Human Beings---to make it easier and legal for citizens to live in Sin without fear of the Legal System).

> Genesis 11:1,4 (KJV)
> 1 "And the whole Earth was one language, and one speech. 4 And they said, Go to, let *us* build a city and a tower, whose top may reach unto Heaven, and let us make *us* a name..."

Tower of Babel would have been a great Human achievement. It symbolized the unity, knowledge and technical skills of the day. It was believed to have been a wonder of the world. Though it was unlikely, with basic materials, they could build a tower even as high as today's skyscrapers!

By Man's standard the pursuit of excellence and unity among the diverse cultures, traditions and religions was a righteous achievement. They wanted to be united under one system and remembered for their contribution to Humanity--perhaps envied.

However the Lord really desired unity of Man with the Holy Spirit--not the unity of the sinful flesh endeavors. The Lord discerned the thoughts of their hearts. He discovered that the tower was merely an Idol, not the progress of engineering--neither was it a tribute to His Goodness and Glory. No, this tower had nothing to do with His Great Name.

The Lord discerned the selfishness of the people. They built the tower to make a "name" for themselves.

Satan seduced the people into a false sense of unity: It was his Babel Syndrome--a flesh inspired greatness marinated in pride, egoism and "us" instead of Him. The purposed unity was only a diversion for the Bent One to *Traffic Iniquity* (like Drug Trafficking).

By there being one language, Sin was readily communicated and ran rampart. In the imaginations of their hearts, nothing would be restrained from them. Wickedness was communicated from individual to family and assimilated the nation. The people had no authority over the Devil: Resistance was futile!

The Holy Spirit begets Spirit and flesh begets flesh. Unity among the masses must also be a Spiritual Unity.

Therefore the *Destiny of Man* was and remains to seek out, lay hold of the spiritual meaning and Purpose of Existence. It involves the individual, family and nation, for the individual must become a *New Creature* accountable to God.

As individuals make up families and families make up the nation --for God is the Father of Human Spirits not nations. God works through individuals to bring change. It's why He ordained marriage and the Family Institution to create Christian Children predestinated to be leaders of nations.

The children also carry out the Will of God concerning the future of the local churches, family, nation and the Human Race. Will our children carry the ball to the Goal Line or fumble it?

We're the descendants of Babel and Israel because we're the Elect. Christ, the Deliverer desires to set us free from Satan's schemes and egotistical entrapments.

The Babel Syndrome continues to this very day. The coming together of all nations is progressively becoming reality. The plan was implement after World War II.

In the New World Order, this age of technology we can travel by ship or airplane to any country in the world. We can make a telephone call via satellite to Russia, China, Egypt or Japan. We can invest our finances in the global markets, foreign stock exchanges at the touch of a button.

It's said by the "movers and the shakers" of the civilized world and the managers and suppliers of the information superhighway, the Internet, that whomever controls the flow of information controls the world.

This is true; those who supply the information can influence Human Beings in a positive or negative way: Truth or Deception. And those who manage the software and information to make the system work also have access to the minds, financial, medical and personal records of those who access or whose statistics are imputed into the system. The right to privacy is becoming an idea of the past; and when information falls into the wrong hands--wicked people, then the system can be a tool of the *Resident Evil* to oppress.

In the New World Order nations are connected electronically, socially, religiously, politically, militarily and financially. The information from all the surveys, researches, criminal investigations, medical, memberships (including church affiliation) and other personal histories are compiled and stored in computers.

Anyone with the technical knowledge or "influence" has access to these records; information isn't totally confidential because at least a dozen people know of it.

Civilization has become another builder of the Tower of Babel. Nothing of any consequences can be transacted without the computer Overseer's authorization and recording of transaction.

To accomplish this, our Social Security Number, bar code number or an electronic implant tracked by global positioning satellites (GPS) will monitor us.

In the hands of the ruthless, civil rights violations, persecutions and imprisonments for resisting the "unity" provided by the New World Order may occur.

For example: Our Credit Cards may be cancelled without warning or explanation, or recomputed to show an inflated debt leading to poor Credit Rating or Bankruptcy; the Mortgage Payment may double or the Bank Foreclose on the home; Christianity may be outlawed and we who confess Jesus as Lord may be denied food, shelter or education for our children; or our children may be taken from us and sent to a State Institution to be "Re-Conformed" to society. It may become law that Christians are unfit parents!

Apostle John wrote concerning the Beast: "And he caused all, both small and great, rich and poor, free and bound, to *receive a mark in their right hand or in their foreheads: and that no Man might buy or sell*, save he that had the mark, or the name of the Beast, or the number of his name [666]" (Revelation 13:16, 17).

the Holy Scriptures state both the rich and poor will be affected by the mark (or Bar Code) of the Beast. The Beast is a Prince Spirit, servant of Satan.

The Movers and the Shakers will themselves be slaves--moved and shaken by a Creature more shrewd than themselves. The Beast will take over and can't be reasoned with, bribed or voted out of office; he will control the New World Order and have access to all the accumulated knowledge about everyone --he needs the stored knowledge because he isn't Omniscient.

In the physical Man devised the system; but the Resident Evil, the Rulers of the Darkness had their hand in its conception, operation and therefore today be found Trafficking Iniquity on many of the Internet web sites.

The Rulers of the Darkness can use the New World Order and its unity to do their bidding. It's like electricity: it can be used to light and heat the home or Capital Punishment; or nuclear energy can be used to generate electricity or vaporize a major city. It depends entirely on who's in control of the technology not necessary what the inventor intended for it to be used.

Again, as Human Beings we contact the External World through our Five Senses: See, Hear, Smell, Taste and Touch. The same way our senses connect and contact the World and those living in it, those living in the World connect and contact us back; they have access to our Mind.

So with the greater access to information and ease in World Communication, it also possible to consume more *Iniquity*, the Tree of Knowledge of Good and Evil.

The website owners with morally legitimate businesses, advertisers and educational concerns are surrounded by ungodly interest --the *Iniquity Traffickers*. The *Iniquity Traffickers* seek to capture the Internet to control the thoughts, motives, desires and standard of conduct--what's "Cool" and what's not.

Before the formation of the Internet, business concerns used newspapers, billboards, television and radio commercials to set trends, "tell" us what to wear, how much to weigh (for woman:

Slim waist, round butt with large breast!), what to eat and drink, brand of Cigarettes to smoke (and what clinic to go to for the best Cancer Treatment! Cigarette Advertisements were taken off television and replaced with Cancer Treatment Hospitals and Centers!)). Their goal is to persuade us to conform to a public image, and thereby getting our hard-earned money.

The Criminologist, Sociologist and other Behavioral Scientists counsel us on what's acceptable behavior in society, what's "normal" for Human Beings to think, feel and believe (being Christian isn't considered normal behavior).

Evolutionist and Philosophers flood the Internet with their opinions; traffickers with Chat Rooms solicit sex; homosexual, Lesbianism and Hetosexual Pornography is plastered over the Internet. But Homosexual and Lesbianism is now considered normal behavior in the Psychiatric Behavior Manuels.

The Psychic Readers receive Millions of Dollars on their sites, at the expense of their own Souls being vexed by Familiar Spirits, and their clients swallowed up by occult demons.

Sin was already entrenched in the world before the invention of radio, telephone, television, New World Order or the Internet. Sin was also in the world before firearms, nuclear weapons, satellites, telemarketing or commercials Nevertheless the Souls of Mankind are being "probed" and "persuaded" by the experts to conform--- not to Christ--- but this world.

Their efforts strengthen the position of the *Resident Evil,* that wars against the Righteousness and Holiness of God and His Wonderful Messiah.

# CHAPTER SEVEN
## CHARMED

Sex and violence has always been a motivator of our Human Psyche. We use sexuality to maneuver one another; sometimes we use sex as a bargaining chip in marriage, business and social relationships--for the opposite sex to do what they wouldn't otherwise agree to. We crave what we cannot or should not have. We need to be emotionally accepted and cuddled often without consideration of morality and decency.

Our fallen nature is such we're aggressive and prone to manipulate people to get what we want. We're also prone to expressions of anger, jealousy, envy and even violence--that's why sex and violence sells at the Movies like chocolates.

These two emotional dispositions are exploited by those who study the Human Mind (including Demonic Spirits) to use knowledge for personal gain.

This is why the Commercialization of Sex and Violence has our eyes riveted to the movie screen. On the screen, it's common to see a ninety-eight percent nude model; in magazines (often completely nude) or billboards and City Buses, advertising personal hygiene products: Perfumes, soaps, tampons, condoms or sleek underwear--even cars, cruises and vacation destinations are advertised using the principles of seduction.

In the movies or television (even video games) it's common to see a victim brutally murdered or an entire family ventilated by robbers armed with automatic weapons; or a "fatal attraction" type relationship; or a divorce turned into neurotically bitter hatred and revenge; or our yearly Halloween specials--frightened teens hacked to death by Freddy; or loving parents murdered in their beds by a deranged son. Violence and gore sells big time!

If alien visitors approached the Earth and monitored our communication channels, they would most likely keep going! If they didn't know the difference between Fiction and Nonfiction programming they'd think we're the most hostile, barbaric and depraved Carbon Units in the Universe. Of course, they would be mistaken--right?

Small children don't know the difference between what's real and what's not; some programs subconsciously disturb children and even give Adults nightmares. Yet most of the knowledge to reason our children acquire comes from television stations, video games, Internet, school, and the streets---with secular parents contributing little or nothing in Spirituality..

Certain programs seduce the emotionally insecure and they more readily conform to the negative images before them. If the program contains terrorism, violence, promiscuity, racism, gangs, cults---information on these subjects is at their fingertips via Computer and the Internet. The mentally unstable, Terrorists and angry people ready supply dangerous information to build bombs, make poisons and build traps to kill people.

Television strives to make their programming realistic and yet it often minimizes the down side of immoral lifestyles to the extent of making them acceptable, alternate lifestyles.

Criminals become bigger than life on the movie screen. The Drug Dealer, Vigilante and Call Girl are glamorous people; and the Drug Addict, Prostitute and Homeless Person are only making a transition in life and will be alright someday; the street gangs and turf wars are necessary for honor, self-esteem and neighborhood pride; life's about getting respect.

Many of our Hollywood Celebrities and famous folks actually believe their publicity, and because they have millions of fans, God is likely among their fans.

Violence in Professional Sports spills over into the private lives of the athletes and their families; even friends and associates suffer the effects of their occasional unholy adrenaline rush.

Famous role models of Screen and Athletic Field are coming before the Judicial System being accused of Rape, Murder, Domestic Violence and Assault.

Then they experience the ultimate Public media embarrassment, convictions for crimes against citizens land many of the role models in prison (including some Church Leaders). Now the Media turns on them and sensationalizes their downfall.

In other areas, Hollywood tries to hide from the public the "real" people who work there--that many of them are miserable, drug, alcohol and sex addicts; many are unstable and suicidal. In the last twenty years, several famous Hollywood personalities were found dead of drug overdoses or Suicide.

So the truth of the matter is, a lot of the people we think should be happy because they have riches, fame, fans, television or political power aren't happy; so why look up to someone who's only pretending to be happy? Looking up to someone who on the outside has a "perfect" body according to Hollywood, but after the camera is off, drink themselves senseless and pop pills like tic tack candies?

What they seek cannot be found anywhere but *In Christ*. From the cradle they have search for the Meaning of their Life and Purpose; but along the way they got Conformed to this world, lost in the world of make believe.

The hard reality is: Crime pays in hard time, and sexual promiscuity can lead to unwanted pregnancies or AIDS; drug abuse can lead to mental illness and death; all the Scientists, Experts, Politicians and Entertainers can't take the place of Jesus Christ.

The philosophy of the Criminal Justice System and the Prison Planners is: "If we build them they will come; we will raise your children for you!" Prisons to warehouse Human Beings until they die is big business. Sounds exactly what Satan would do.

The majority of the finances for Drug Programs, Homeless Shelters, Crisis Intervention, Public Schools and Social Services has gone to building new prisons (what hasn't been diverted to Homeland Security, War On Terror, and Foreign Aid).

A dysfunctional environment causes instability in the home. many teenagers turn to coping devices such as cigarettes, Marijuana, liquor, using drugs, sex and violence to rebel against authority. Their values are of the world, not according to the Word of

Word of God. But if the children grow up and conform too well to the ways of the world and become too dangerous, the prison system has a bunk for them!

Anyone who swallows enough water will drown; and too much world can kill. The world pickles the brain, bankrupts our Soul and binds us with ball and chain to the hard Earth. We struggle but can't get free. But whom the Son has set free is free indeed.

As children we were very impressionable too. Whatever we were taught at an early age became the foundation everything else was built upon. We spent hours watching immoral acts: violent cartoons, after school shows and prime time entertainment that lacked Biblical Morality. Nevertheless, it was introduced and assimilated by our young minds.

Later, we couldn't wait to smoke our first cigarette, drink beer, kiss romantically etc... This programming was explicitly formulated to get our attention, conform our precious minds to what was acceptable and expected of us; what was considered normal behavior in our material-minded, aggressively-violent, self-gratifying, greed-oriented world owned by Satan!

For the above reasons many Teenagers are in a pursuit of fame (even if it requires shooting their Classmates and themselves). They want to protest the years of being in subjection to parents, teachers and society: They're in Rebellion.

Fame and Power is the reason that Wicca, a satanic cult of Witches and Warlocks is the fastest growing practice among Teenagers. It's strange why a traditionally "parent-hating" age group resisting parental authority that was given by God would submit to yet another form of authority given by the Devil!

In general, Teenagers have very little authority in the home. The parents make all the important decisions. Even when the Teenager is allowed to participate in an important decision the parents, who earn the money have the final decision.

It's part of the reason that Wicca appeals to the young. It promises them power to Cast Spells and Incantations to control people. In traditional family life, society and Church, they can't have such power.

The delusion of authority they seek arrives. Now they feel important, in control of their lives--even the lives of others, but it's only an illusion.

The so-called good Samaritan witches the television shows portray are inconsistent with the Divine Scriptural Revelations concerning Witchcraft and those who practice it. The real goal of the *Resident Evil* using the Human practitioner is the Manipulation, Intimidation and Domination by using fear against parents, teachers, classmates and anyone who gets in the way. To the occultist (and Terrorists), Fear equals power and power equals control--thus the goal is to Dominate and Proselytize followers to help Traffic Iniquity.

The rituals and symbols appeal to the young because the children have been seeing them on television and as toys all their lives. The young are indoctrinated with forms and symbols of "detestable objects" such as the troll, Fairy, frog, owl, snake, Ouija Board, Magic Wand, rabbit's foot, good-luck charms, demon, monster dolls and African Voodoo Masks that represent evil, the Supernatural Realm and its Rulers.

The ritualistic demands are made by the Evil Spirits behind the physical curtain. As the interest and participation becomes more intense, the small animal sacrifices aren't enough and larger animals. Sometimes Human Babies are sacrificed to make the incantations work.

By degrees the familiar and personality-altering Unclean Spirits take control of the Wiccans, and stronger Unclean Spirits enter into their Psyche to live and control the Mind. Then Unclean Spirits (possibly a legion) enter and make their habitation in the Wiccan; the Unclean Spirits talk between themselves and the Wiccans hears voices as the Unclean Spirits argue, fight and make daily decisions concerning how they will use the Wiccan to precipitate evil.

As the practice of Wicca continues the Teenager experiences irrational and emotional changes due to the abundance of foreign personalities living in his psyche. Unusual behavioral patterns emerge as the insidious wills of the Evil Spirits manifest in the eternal world; the psychic door being pried open, the subconscious mind becomes compromised to allow hallucinations, paranoia, depression, abominations such as the drinking of blood, eating raw flesh, sexual perversions, cravings to inflict and/or receive torture and punishment to satisfy some twisted grace.

The Unclean Spirits manipulates the Teenager into performing a pledge of obedience to the Dark Side: Perhaps kill one or more of their parents, brother or sister; or kill their classmates and/or themselves.

The controlling Unclean Spirits become entrenched in the thinking and personality of the Teenager's life the Teenager loses self-control, and may wind up permanently confined in a Mental Institution or dead.

Every year, thousands of the people are missing as victims of Human Sacrifices. Satan is an equal opportunity employer; he's also an equal opportunity destroyer.

Controlling Spirits have always been among us. Even in Old Testament times these Evil Spirits used Human Beings to control the nations of the world. As stated earlier, Witchcraft and other "Mystery Schools" including the "High Places" of the past have indoctrinated children into the art of practicing evil.

But children, as the Bible shows us, aren't the only ones susceptible to the lure of evil; these forbidden arts have been passed down by Adults.

God's Word has also been handed down through time to combat the forces of Darkness. God said in Exodus 22:18, "You shall not allow a Witch to live." The point is clear (Under the New Testament Covenant of Grace through Repentance and Faith, we don't kill but convert them. In the Old Testament they were killed and went to Sheol, the After Life; today if they were killed, they would go to Hell.) that the Black Arts by whatever modern name given them, remains the same in God's eyes and will not be tolerated.

> Deuteronomy 4:19 18:12 (Amp. Bible)
> 19 "And beware lest you lift up your eyes to the heavens, and when you see the sun, moon, and stars, even all the host of the heavens, you be drawn away and worship them...12 for all who do these things are an abomination to the Lord, and it is because of these abominable practices..."

From these Scriptures we learn that God wants us to be faithful and devoted to the Worship of Him, to trust in His ability to protect and provide for us. When we petition the Dark Side, Satan's area of control to supply our needs we automatically declare and demonstrate our lack of confidence and Faith in the Father; and by seeking Psychic Powers that God considers abominable practices is willful Rebellion.

The Lord God wants us to live in the sunshine not the shadows. Whereas Witchcraft has many tentacles including idols, people, and materialism. Let's not be fooled by name-swapping or dropping: The package is the same. If for some reason we need to know the future we must not ask the Psychics but entreat God or one of his Prophets.

Samuel told King Saul the Word of the Lord concerning Witchcraft. He said, "For Rebellion is as the Sin of Witchcraft, and Stubbornness is as Idolatry and Teraphim (household good-luck images). because you have rejected the Word of the Lord..."

Witchcraft and Rebellion are demonic twins.

> 1 Samuel 28:3,7,11 (Amp. Bible)
> 3 "Now Samuel was dead, and all Israel had mourned...
> 7 Then Saul said to his servants, Find me a woman who is a Medium [between the living and the dead)...11 The woman said, Whom shall I bring up [from Sheol] for you? He said, Bring up Samuel for me."

King Saul learned the hard way that God means what He says. It's the same lesson Adam and Eve failed; it's the same lesson that all Mankind fails: That lesson is OBEDIENCE.

King Saul was anointed the first King of Israel. It was God who picked him out from among his brothers and the entire nation of Israel. Several times Saul disobeyed God but the last time was just that. Instead of Saul rekindling his Love and Faith in God, petitioning His throne for Forgiveness and guidance, Saul petitioned a Witch and disturbed the eternal rest of one of God's blessed Saints.

Samuel rebuked Saul for bringing him up from Sheol, the place reserved in that era for the safe keeping of Souls. While Samuel was there with Saul he gave Saul the information, and also told him things he didn't want to hear.

The Philistines were also the Lord's enemy. God would've helped Saul conquer the Philistines. But Saul was too proud to go to God concerning the Nation or his own Repentance; instead he went to God's enemy, the Devil, a Witch, an abomination to His authority; Saul communicated with the dead rather than the Living God, thus sidestepping God and glorifying the resources of His enemy.

Even today Familiar Spirits on the other side of the veil have information about our past, present and future--even world events. These are the Familiar Spirits the Psychics contact; whereas, the majority of Psychics have at least one Demonic Spirit living inside them, using them to Channel into the world.

But to consult a Psychic would entangle us in their Rebellious lifestyle, bind us to share in their *Destiny*, their fate, perhaps causing our *Destiny* as the predestined Elect of God, the Gifts and Calling of the Holy Spirit in our lives not to be fulfilled.

Our *Destiny* could become such as we really wouldn't enjoy living it. God must always have the ultimate say in the future of the Christian. The Psychics are not God neither do they work for Him.

They are liars and deceive us into accepting them as the "Voice of God" when in fact they are the Voice of Satan. God communicates by His Holy Spirit; working in us, they're called

Spiritual Gifts. The Revelation Gifts are: Prophecy, Word of Wisdom, Word of Knowledge and Discerning of Spirits.

> 2 Chronicles 33:1-3,6,7 (Amp. Bible)
> 1 "Manasseh was Twelve Years Old when he began to reign, and he reigned Fifty-Five Years in Jerusalem. 2 but he did evil in the Lord's sight...3 for he built again the [idolatrous) High Places... 6 and he burned his children as an offering [to his god]...and practiced Soothsaying, Augury, and Sorcery, and dealt with Mediums and Wizards...provoking Him to anger."

King Manasseh was a very sick man. He wasn't born that way but learned about Idols and Witchcraft from the Elders and travelers from foreign lands. The religions of the High Places of worship came from Israel's conformity to the society of their captors; but the actual construction in Israel of these High Places was Israel's downfall; other Strange Fire types of worship originated in the nations that the Lord brought judgment upon by using Israel to conquer them. Unfortunately, Manasseh brought the Black Arts to an all-time low.

The king was worse than the heathens! He practiced all types of Dark Arts, sacrificed his own children to the flames and provoked the anger of God.

Perhaps, when Manasseh first began he thought the other religions were "alternate" forms of worshipping God--that all worship is alike. But that deception cost him and Israel plenty--because the Devil lied to him. The devil can't be trusted; it's like giving a known thief money to hold. The only roads that are alike lead to many forms of misery and eventual destruction. Worshipping God is a Narrow Road.

> 2 Kings. 23:24 (Amp. Bible)
> 24 Moreover, Josiah put away the Mediums, the Wizards, the Teraphim (household gods), the Idols, and all the Ab-

ominations that were seen in Judah and in Jerusalem, that he might establish the Words of the Law written in the Book..."

"Josiah was Eight Years Old when he began his Thirty-One Year reign in Jerusalem" (2 Kings 22:1). At Eight Years Old Josiah wasn't mature enough to lead the Nation of Israel. His "appointed" Advisors and Counselors tutored him on how to govern.

The previous kings including Solomon, Ahab and Manasseh caused Israel to Sin. They were the ones who built the High Places and Psychic Arts thrived causing the Lord's anger to burn hot against them. It was apparent most of Josiah's Counselors were from the previous Administration and their advice tainted.

Nevertheless when Josiah matured he knew in his Soul that something was terribly wrong with the Nation of Israel. When he discovered the Word of God, he immediately surrendered, made a Covenant with God not to allow Satan to use him to rule Israel from behind the veil.

The bold king immediately initiated a nationwide reform. He pulled down the Idols at the High Places. He yanked the false gods out of the Lord's House and pulverized them. He tore down the houses of the Male Prostitutes which were by the Lord's House (2 Kings 23:7). Josiah was determined to deliver Israel.

Josiah and Manasseh were both children when they became kings. Both had the opportunity to serve or not to serve God; they had the will and option to allow or disallow Satan to corrupt their lives and Nation.

Manasseh chose for himself and Israel the idolatrous life of Satanic Worship and Psychic Arts; while Josiah Covenanted with the Lord and the Lord strengthened him to perform His Word. Again, God reestablished a Name for Himself in Israel.

By putting an end to the Psychic Arts, Josiah slammed the door in Satan's face. Satan's works grieved the Holy Spirit.

Today the Church (and the Nation) is in a battle against Witchcraft. The Psychics claim we don't need God and whatevever *Destiny* He planned. All we need is to "activate" the "power within us; take control over our own *Destiny,* over the Psychic Soul Powers within--- and this control will change the environment within and without; or, seek the assistance of a "Spirit Guide" to help us make important life decisions.

Some claim that Numerology and the Astrology of the stars and planets hold the key to our happiness and well being. Fate, Karma, Luck, Charms, Incantations, Spells, Psychic Readings, the Universe--- are common terms used to describe getting control over our lives.

Many cults want us to believe that the goal of life is to be swallowed up (at-one-with) the Universe or nature. Here, our Individuality and Free Will is forfeited to some unknown place or force called the "Universe," or "Nature," which is actually another trick for selling our Soul to Satan.

However, God is a Person, the Supreme Being--not the Universe or Nature; He's the Creator not the created. He gave us Free Will and won't accept it back. He desires that we use our Free Will to seek Him and not to give it up to Satan. The reason why the cults want us to give up our Free Will is so they can Manipulate, Dominate and use us; to take our hard-earned money and squander it; to abuse us and our family members with twisted moral values often driven by the Lust of the Flesh.

This is why Cult Leaders, usually Male, promote sexual promiscuity and perversions--to satisfy their flesh; also cutting, blood lettings, sacrifices, militant stockpiling of weapons and often encourage mass suicides when confronted by Authority.

The Lord Jesus Christ wants to clean up our lives and then the Nation. He desires a people zealous to do good works. He has been Patient and Longsuffering with our infatuations, unholy and detestable ways and objects of demonic praise and worship.

> Acts 8:9, 13 (Amp. Bible)
> 9 "There was a man named Simon, who formally practiced Magic Arts in the city... 13 Even Simon him-

self believed [ adhered to, trust in, and relied on the teaching of Philip], and after being Baptized, devoted himself constantly to him. and seeing Signs and Miracles of great power performed, he was utterly amazed."

Philip the Deacon [not the Apostle] went down to the City of Samaria and preached the Gospel to the Gentiles. By the Holy Spirit, Philip also performed Miracles, Signs and Wonders. He cast out Unclean Spirits and Healed a lot of people, and because of this, there was great joy in the city.

The people believed the Word and the Kingdom of God manifested; wherever the Kingdom of God is, Demons and Diseases are cast out. There is no Fellowship between Christ and Satan.

In the city was a man named Simon. He was a Sorcerer who bewitched the people with extraordinary feats of Magic. Many of the Officials were afraid of him, others respected him for he told them that he represented the Great Power of God.

When Philip arrived, the Anointed Spirit of God arrived in him. Simon was impressed and utterly amazed by what the Holy Spirit achieved through Philip; Simon's Magic was of the past, Simon believed the Word of God, was *Water Baptized* and Born Again (v.13). He followed Philip around, learned about Jesus Christ and observed the Acts of the Holy Spirit.

Shortly afterwards the Apostles came down from Jerusalem to bless the Believers with the **Baptism in the Holy Spirit** .

Through Repentance and Faith in Jesus Christ, Salvation and the Holy Spirit came to the Believers; Now the Apostles brought an additional Blessing, the Second work of Grace, an extremely important Anointing of Power for Service. It's one thing to be Saved, quite another to Serve with Holy Spirit Power.

However, when Simon saw and heard the Holy Spirit come upon the people--the speaking in *Other Tongues and Prophecy Manifestations* (Acts 2:4), he offered to pay the Apostles to give him the power to administer this *Baptism*. To his dismay, Simon received an ear full rebuke from Peter. The Apostle discerned the

Demonic Spirits still within Simon. Although Simon Believed in Christ, was indwelled in the Human Spirit by Christ's Holy Spirit, Simon's Soul Body remained "compromised" because of his previous lifestyle.

This previous lifestyle, the philosophy he was accustomed to, became a pitfall. It was the Old Way of thinking standing in the path of the New Way of thinking.

"Grant me this Power and Authority" (v.19) is what Simon requested. The request sounded reasonable until the Holy Spirit in Peter discerned Simon's Soul. There was more involved inside of Simon than came out his mouth. Simon said he wanted to lay his hands on others so they could receive the *Baptism in the Holy Spirit*.

But in his heart the Unclean Spirits coveted the glee of having additional Authority, Power and Fame. Simon had the cover pulled off of him! He was naked and exposed to Apostle Peter's stare.

Apostle Peter foretold destruction of Simon's money and him too. Peter saw a heart needing Repentance of the depravity, wickedness, bitterness, the bond forged by an Oath, a Covenant.

Simon needed Deliverance, the yoke and Curse removed from his Soul's neck. He was a Born Again Christian. But Simon was still controlled by the Evil Spirits, who in previous years worked Magic through him. He could thank God that Apostle Peter told him of his condition; and the of Grace and Mercy Lord would forgive and deliver him upon Simon's earnest petition.

Salvation and Regeneration are common terms used to describe the same thing---the New Birth. After Regeneration, Sanctification begins; it's the Process the Holy Spirit uses to change us into the Image (Character and Likeness) of Jesus Christ; this is a *life-long process*, and mainly deals with the Soul-Mind arena. (that's how altogether *other* we are compared to Jesus Christ).

Included in the *lifelong process* of Sanctification, among other benefits, is Deliverance. Now, Deliverance is the casting out of Evil Spirits including Occult Demons residing in the Soul and Physical Bodies. (the Human Spirit is occupied by the Holy Spirit).

Sicknesses, Diseases and Emotional Instabilities are often attributed to Unclean Spirits resident in the Soul or Physical Bodies; sometimes Unclean Spirits attach themselves outside the Body.

Salvation is the New Birth and the New Birth involves the Recreation and Resurrection of the Human Spirit by the indwelling Holy Spirit. Whereas, Deliverance involves the Soul and Physical Bodies receiving a sudden "blast" of the Holy Spirit to dislodge and drive out deep-rooted controlling Demon Spirits.

Many times simultaneously with the New Birth, Deliverance from Demon Spirits, Addictions, Sicknesses and Diseases occurs; but most of the time complete Deliverance comes later.

Ignorance or *avoidance of Deliverance* is the reason why "professed" Christians habitual Sin, have mental and emotional disturbances in their lives; some have recurring nightmares. Also being a past practitioner in such Psychic Arts as Astral Projection, Soul Travel and Transcendental Meditation (and several other Eastern Cult Techniques said to relax the Mind and Body, defile our Being.)

Religious Tradition has most Christians believing that Receiving Jesus Christ as Savior and Lord is all there is.. So if problems persist, we must not be Saved--that's a lie from the pit of Hell. Deliverance is the answer to persistent struggles against vices, additions, emotional disturbances and other torments within us. Without the Provisions of Deliverance guilt, shame, rejection and other soul-crippling emotions, Defiling Spirits would keep us in bondage to the past forever; the misery, guilt and shame of and habitually missing the mark could drive us away from Christianity, and Jesus Christ who loves us, and has already purchased Deliverance for us at the Redeeming Cross.

Therefore, God has called Christians into the Ministry of Divine Healing and Deliverance. Earnestly seek these Ministries.

> Acts 19:11 (Amp. Bible)
> 11 "And God did *unusual and extraordinary* Miracles by the hands of Paul."

When the Word of God is preached, and Faith is present, it's confirmed by Signs and Wonders (Mark 16:20). God the Holy Spirit used Paul to bring to nothing the Forces of Darkness bewitching the citizens of Ephesus. The city was a stronghold of Demonic Cults.

The Seven Sons of Sceva were almost ripped apart by Demons as these Jews attempted to imitate Paul in casting out Evil Spirits (Acts 19:13-16). The Evil Spirits shrieked in fear at the Name of Jesus and Paul's Authority to use that Name; but the Sons of Sceva weren't Christians and therefore not Authorized to use His Name. The Evil Spirits beat the clothes off them!

The Anointing inherited in the Word destroyed yokes and bondages throughout the city. People were Born Again, *Baptized in the Holy Spirit, Healed and Delivered* in miraculous ways.

The Holy Spirit manifested throughout the city and brought Repentance --that convincing in the heart concerning Sin, Righteousness and Judgment. Many were converted from Witchcraft to Christianity.

As a demonstration of their new found *Destiny,* what Christ had done in their lives, they burned their Psychic Arts Books. These books cost them a boatload of money; these same books would have cost them more than money could buy: The practice of Witchcraft would've sent their Souls straight to Hell.

The Psychic Arts are part of the reason why Hell has been enlarged. There awaits a special and horrible fate reserved for the Witches and Sorcerers.

Today we're inclined to hold on to the past, the familiar for sentimental or security reasons. We fail to consider t our Past can influence our Presence walk with the Lord, because we've not letting go of the abominable practices He loathes.

Christians who call upon Psychics, Astrologers and participate in Séances, Ouija board or Tarot cards o err from the Faith.

Paul wrote to the Galatians and asked: "0 foolish Galatians, who has bewitched you, that you should not obey the truth?" (Galatians 3:1-3).

# CHAPTER EIGHT
## THE ANOINTING DESTROYS THE YOKE

> Luke 17:12,13, (Amp. Bible)
> 12 "and He was going into one village, He was met by ten Lepers, who stood at a distance. 13 and they raised their voices and called, Jesus, Master take Pity and have Mercy on us!"

During Jesus' Ministry He often walked among enormous crowds of people whose *Destiny* seemed bleak. But a Word from the Lord, a touch from the Master's hand, changed their entire life.

The multitudes made demands upon His time and Anointing. In this particular instance, ten Lepers voiced their agony at being tormented by a debilitating disease and forced to live a rejected, subhuman, outcast existence.

They wailed the cry that only the terminally afflicted can, and above the usual noise of the crowd. They maintained a distance, because the Mosaic Law forbade a Leper from coming within reasonable distance of healthy people, so the lepers were considerable distance away. Yet because of their urgency, they cried and Jesus heard them. "Have mercy and pity on us!"

Jesus loved them and declared their Healing. He told them to verify it with the Priest, who had the authority to pronounce them Clean. But before they got to the Priest they were Healed.

The Anointed Word healed all ten Lepers but only one allowed the changing power to pass through the flesh and affect his Soul. In his heart this lone Leper wanted more from God and life than a Physical Healing---HE WANTED A GOOD DESTINY!

He wanted a Personal Relationship with the Christ the Healer. Being physically fit and *Spiritually Dead* wasn't his idea of being set free. He humbled himself before Jesus, the Mercy Seat, and Worshipped Him. Then he Thanked and Praised Jesus.

The Joy of the Lord became his Strength. He stretched out on the ground before Jesus and fervently offered unto Him the sacrifice of Praise and the fruit of his lips giving thanks unto His Holy Name.

The Holy Spirit really changed his life, attitude and perspective towards God. He believed his disease originated because of his Sins (Job was also told this by his friends), that God was punishing him: The Priest said that Leprosy was a sure sign of Condemnation. But Jesus showed him that it was God's will to Heal him--and it wasn't God, but an Unclean Spirit that made him Diseased!

Whereas, the other nine, seeing they were healed, went their way satisfied with the Physical Healing. They gave no indication of Thanks, Praise or Testimony to the "Pity and Mercy" they asked for and received from Jehovah-Elohim and His Messiah.

Perhaps they went into the city to their families, or got cleaned up and went out on the town for an Evening of indulgence, then returned to a life of Darkness.

They didn't experience what the lone Samaritan did, for if they had they would've returned and given Thanks. They took for granted the Miracles. Their physical lives were prolonged for a season but one day they would actually die.

The nine Lepers had an opportunity to secure the New Birth, the Promise (after Jesus Resurrected) of Eternal life, the Resurrection from the Dead.

Samaritans were considered outcasts and dogs. But King Solomon wrote that "a living dog is better than a dead lion" (Ecclesiastes 9:4). This Samaritan was that live dog among nine dead lions and a multitude of self-righteous, Spiritually Dead Jews.

Sometimes we are loud to acquire blessings from God but get quiet on Him when it comes time to give thanks. We must submit to the life-changing power of the Holy Spirit. God not only wants to Heal our Physical Body but our Soul, with its ungrateful and selfish attitudes.

We all have character flaws, imperfections and bad habits from being nurtured in this fallen world. However, there's no reason why we should conceal and perpetrate fraudulent "holiness" when we can expose and be cleansed of Unclean Spirits. We shouldn't willfully walk in agreement with Devils. Ignorance isn't bliss; we mustn't shorten the Hand of God. Accept His Deliverance. Then "Give thanks unto Him and bless His Name" (Psalms 100:4).

As the Redeemed we must claim the Promises of God. These Promises don't help us because they are available—we must claim them, voice our needs then return, like the Leper, and lay at Jesus' feet, thanking Him for the blessings.

> Luke 18:35,38,42,43 (Amp. Bible)
> 35 "...a blind man was sitting by the roadside begging. 38 And he shouted, saying, Jesus, Son of David, take *Pity* and have *Mercy* on me! 42 And Jesus said to him, receive your sight! Your *Faith* (your trust and confidence that spring from your *Faith* in God) has *Healed* you. 43 And instantly he received his sight and began to follow Jesus, Recognizing, Praising, and Honoring God..."

Again a man's Faith in Jesus had gotten him the victory over the infirmities of the flesh, and warmed his lost Soul to the possibilities in offering the sacrifice of Praise and Worship. The man was blind but he wasn't crazy. He knew about the Name, the Reputation of Jesus; he knew the Son of David was in the land-- and where the Kingdom is, Healing would follow.

The crowd--those religious folks demanded that he kept quiet. They felt it was undignified to beg and plead in public. But they thought that because they could see! As far as the blind man was concerned, he had nothing to lose, so he didn't care what they thought. He knew what he wanted and pressed into the kingdom to receive his blessing.

Because of his persistence and Faith, he was a true son of Abraham and entitled by Covenant Relationship to be Healed. He staked his Claim to the Promises, God's Covenant with Abraham and his Descendants. These great Promises were as good for him

Centuries later, as they were the day God Promised them. In return, the blind man Glorified and Magnified God; then he continued with Jesus. His Faith brought forth action and a Spiritual Relationship with the Messiah. In more ways than one his eyes were opened and Light flooded his entire being.

> John 3:18,19 (Amp. Bible)
> 18 "He who Believes in Him [who clings to, trust in, relies on Him] is not Judged [he who trust in Him never comes up for Judgment; for him there is no Rejection, no Condemnation --he incurs no Damnation]; but he who does not Believe [cleave to, rely on, trust in Him] is Judged already [he has already been Convicted and has already received his Sentence] because he has not Believed in and trusted in the Name of the Only Begotten Son [he is condemned for refusing to let his trust rest in Christ's Name]. 19 the [basis of the] Judgment (Indictment, the Test by which men are Judged, the Ground for the Sentence) lies in this: the Light (Christ) has come into the world, and people have loved the Darkness rather than and more than the Light, for their works (deeds) were evil."

The above Scriptures sums up Heavenly Court Case against un-regenerated, Non-Christian Man, and how he can escape the false *Destiny* thrust upon him by the Prince of Darkness, also escape the Final Judgment and Eternal Internship in Hell; and enter into his *Appointed Destiny* and *Rendezvous* with Jesus Christ at the Throne of God.

Spiritual Blindness is worst than Physical Blindness. Once the decision was made to accept Jesus Christ as our Personal Lord and Savior the New Birth satisfied the Indictment for refusing to come to the Light. We're seated on the Mercy Seat, at the Throne of Grace; whereas Physical Blindness cannot hinder us from "seeing" the Kingdom and entering into its glorious splendor.

For it's said that none are so blind as those who refuse to see.

> Luke 19:2-5, (Amp. Bible)
> 2 "And there was a man called Zacchaeus, a Chief Tax Collector, and [he was] rich. 3 And he was trying to see Jesus...but he could not, on account of the crowd became he was small in stature. 4 So he ran ahead and climbed up in a sycamore tree... 5 And when Jesus reached the place, He looked up and said to him, Zacchaeus, hurry and come down..."

"Zacchaeus, hurry and come down", was Jesus' Greeting. "Salvation has come to you and your family; the Kingdom of Heaven is at hand!"

Zacchaeus was a Tax Collector and a very hated man. He worked against his own people as the Romans' Chief Tax Collector. In the process of collecting revenue, he had gotten rich by making fraudulent claims, extortions, accusations and schemes. No one considered him "worthy" to even approach Jesus, let alone the Master going to his house. To them Zacchaeus was a devoted sinner, the typical bottom-of-the-barrel traitor.

When Zacchaeus knew that Jesus was in the area he felt something change inside him. Someplace in his Soul a thick and high wall fell down. For the first time in a long time he didn't consider--or even care how much the crowd hated him, that his Authority and wealth came at their suffering and expense; or he could've paid men to clear him a path to Jesus.

He swallowed his pride, ran ahead and climbed a tree. As he climbed he didn't care how undignified or peculiar it looked: A grown, wealthy midget, pegged as a traitorous, arrogant rogue, perched up in a tree for all to see.

Jesus saw him a true son of Abraham. Without Jesus asking, Zacchaeus volunteered to give half his wealth and right the wrongs of his tax collecting. He affirmed with his mouth what the Spirit of Christ had done in his heart —plotted a New Course for

for his life, one that included Jesus. Jesus called him a son.

Zacchaeus wasn't the same Man he was an hour ago. From the outside he looked the same but God changed his inner Man. He and his entire family was changed; for the witness of the change was his Repentance and Confession of Obedience and Faith, followed by his works, the action of his words.

Certainly his family saw the change in him as he came in the door with the famed Jesus of Nazareth. Because of the change in Zacchaeus the other members of his household also Believed in the Message of Salvation. Truly when a greedy man gives half his money to the poor an Emergency Heart Transplant has taken place!

We all can learn from the Scriptures and look at the success of those who pleased God. The Word was given to us to profit and step up higher into Glory. We must consider the Lord Jesus Christ and not consider our present limitations or the opinions of others. People don't have a Heaven or Hell to put us in. In fact, they're running for their own lives! Let the Holy Spirit lead.

We consider the brightness of His Glory and image of the Person of Jesus Christ. In Him resides the fullness of the Godhead Bodily (now in Glorified Body). And "as many as received Him, to them gave He Power (Authority, Right) to become the Sons of God, even to them who Believe on His Name. Which were born, not of blood, nor the will of the flesh, nor of the will of Man, but of God" (John 1:12,13).

The Word, the Christ of God became flesh and pitched His tent among us. Jesus Christ brought Grace and Truth into an unstable world of bondage. He brought fullness and declared for all times the Father's inexhaustible Love and Forgiveness.

He brought back to Creation the Yoke-Destroying, Burden-Bearing, Devil-Stomping Anointing. Not only did Christ bring the Anointing but delegated the Anointing upon whosoever Believes in, cleaves to, trusts in and relies on Him.

As Children of God we're truly blessed. Jesus said, "I have come that they might have Life, and that they might have it more abundantly" (John 10:10). The abundant Life of being Born Again and led by the Holy Spirit is the Victorious Life.

Jesus didn't come here to be a Lawman--- like in the Old American West---to give us more laws and rules to live by. Instead He gave us Authority and Power; and a God-Breathed Lifestyle that He helps us to live. He's not a Minister of Condemnation but a Life-giving Spirit.

He also came to complete the Holy Bible. The Bible is the Revelation, the Word of God; it's not the opinions of Jesus of Nazareth, the Prophets or Apostles. The Bible and the Word of God are inseparable and immutable. Its words help us grasp with our Intellect, Emotions, Imagination and Will the Person and unity of the Trinity and our place in it.

"And you shall know the Truth, and the Truth shall make you free" (John 8:32). Without the Word, the Truth (Christ) would be an unsolved Mystery, and Satan, who resists the Truth, would forever reign lord of our lives.

No one would ever know or experience the Life of the Spirit, freedom from the torments and slavery of sin, nor the Father's fiery love and Jesus Christ whom He has sent. Without the hearing of the Word, we wouldn't have considered the Chief Apostle and High Priest of our Faith--and lost out big time on the countless blessings heaped upon blessings, and favor upon favor, and gifts upon gifts.

With the Anointing we don't consider the outward appearances and circumstances, the being "as grasshoppers in our own eyes." *Syndrome.* We consider Jesus Christ who sits upon the Heavenly Throne; and who are they that sit with Him in the heavenly places? The Church of Jesus Christ.

It's Jesus Christ who "Himself" took our infirmities, and bare our sicknesses" (Matthew 8:17). Isaiah and the Apostles only wrote about our Sicknesses and Diseases, but Jesus actually took them away. In this, Jesus demonstrated the Will of God concerning Delivering our Spirit, Souls, and Body.

Our Savior said, "The words that I speak to you are Spirit, and they are Life. His words are impregnated with Elohim-Life, Implosive, Fortified with Divine Authority and won't return to Him void but shall accomplish His Will. The Living Word is in us. "Christ in you, the Hope of Glory" (Colossians 1:27).

This same Word was in the beginning with God; all things were made by Him. this Word was made flesh; this identical Word/Christ also dwells in us, bringing us into the Trinity, the Elohim Unity.

The Unity that Jesus Christ prayed for wasn't only for His Apostles but included all those born of the Holy Spirit. With Pentecost, the **Dispensation of Grace,** the Church ushered in.

The Adoption of Children brought forth the manifestation of God's Salvation Plan and the answer to Jesus' prayer. He prayed into being the perfect Will of God and caused the Holy Spirit to break through the veil into Creation. The Unity the Father and Son share was given to us to form the Commonalty: Father/Son-Church/ Holy Spirit.

"Therefore if any Man be in Christ, he is a New Creature (Creation/Species); old things are passed away; behold all things are become new" (2 Corinthians 5:17). We have become a "New Species". Our Human Spirit is no longer the same. If we allow *Sanctification* to fully run its course, we'll also become new in Soul and Physical Body, will undergo healings and renewed strength. We would live longer and produce more godly fruit.

Being *In Christ* isn't being put on the Church Role or attendance in Bible College, but being Adopted through the Holy Spirit's Adoption Agency. He puts our hands in God's hands.

As Children of the Resurrection, God is truly our Father (John 8:44). After the New Birth we aren't the same on the inside as before; we have a new nature, position, Purpose and *Destiny*. Our "Inward man is renewed day by day" (2 Corinthians 4:16). The "*hidden Man of the heart*" (1 Peter 3:4) has survived the plot of the Enemy. Wherefore, "he that is joined to the Lord is One Spirit" (Corinthians 6:17).

# CHAPTER NINE
## DELIVERANCE

Adam was entrusted with the Word of God. The Word of God was every word that proceeded out of God's mouth. Among these words were commands: "Be fruitful and multiply and replenish the Earth, and subdue it; and have Dominion..." (Genesis 1:28). Thus because of the Word of God, Adam reigned as god of this world.

Since it was the results of God's Word that Adam was given Dominion and Authority, it was also the disobeying of God's Word that ultimately caused Adam to lose his Dominion and Authority. The modus operandi of the Word hasn't changed.

Therefore, it's our Faith in God's Word that maintains an activation of His Word in our lives. The *Faith of God* is inherited in His Word. Our Faith must unite with the Faith inherited in the Word to bring it to pass in our lives. In short, we must Agree with the Word of God.

> Romans 4:18-21 (Amp. Bible)
> 18 "[For Abraham, Human reason for] Hope being gone, hoped in Faith that he should become the father of many nations, as he had been Promised, So [numberless] shall your Descendants be."

The life of Abraham was not a life without Temptations and Controversy. His story wasn't recorded in the Holy Bible because he was perfect, a faultless example, or even that he fathered a child when he was "as good as dead" because of his age.

Abraham wasn't known because Sarah's womb was barren, and the miracle that God performed in restoring her womb; or his wife, Sarah was so beautiful that King Abimelech was dazzled and wanted her. No, Abraham was known for his Faith in God.

Abraham believed God was able and willing to keep His Promises. Abraham didn't lean on his natural talents, his physical appearance, wealth, community ties or what other people believed, but depended on God who could do exceeding and abundantly above all he could ask or think.

"Abraham believed God and it was counted unto him for Righteousness" (Romans 4:3). Abraham believed in Him who Justifies (Declared Not Guilty through Faith) the ungodly (Romans 4:5). Abraham wasn't perfect but served a perfect God, who Justified him by his Faith, not works, and counted his Faith as righteousness (Romans 4:22).

"Therefore being Justified by Faith, we have Peace with God through our Lord Jesus Christ" (Romans 4:25). The Peace we enjoy was purchased at the Cross. Salvation, Sanctification, Healing and Deliverance was purchased by the Blood of Jesus Christ. It's by Faith that we appropriate, lay claim to the Dominion Christ won back for us.

As only by Faith Adam, Abraham, the Prophets and Jesus pleased God; and the Avenue of Faith has not changed.

*Spiritual Laws* apply to everyone, in the same way Gravity affect us and our neighbors all over the world.

"But without Faith it is IMPOSSIBLE TO PLEASE HIM; for he that comes to God must *Believe* that He is, and that He is a rewarder of them that diligently seek Him" (Hebrews 11:6).

We must first Believe in the Promises of God, that He will keep His Promises. These are the two immutable concepts: God has made Promises and God cannot lie.

> Isaiah. 10:27  59:19
> 27 "and it shall come to pass in that day, that his [Satan's] burden shall be taken away from off your shoulders, and his yoke from off your [our] neck, and the yoke shall be destroyed because of the Anointing. 19 when the enemy [Satan] shall come in, like a flood the Spirit of the Lord shall lift up a standard against him."

The yoke-destroying power of the Anointing will drive out the Enemy. Like a flood, the Spirit of the Lord will lift up the Heavenly Standard of Righteousness and bring about Peace, Healings, Mental Stability and Deliverance from the torments, freedom from the molestation of demonic spirits. His promises are available to whosoever will ask in Jesus' Name.

When the Enemy comes in he comes to stay. It's not a visit but an Occupation; it's not to steal our television, jewelry or sports car--but our Health, Soul-Mind and Human Spirit. He came to steal, kill and destroy everything of eternal weight in Glory. The thief of our Peace, Tranquility, Rest and Love is his target.

But God! "He Delivers and Rescues, and works Signs and Wonders in the Heaven and in the Earth, who has delivered Daniel from the Power of the Lions" (Daniel 6:27).

Daniel was delivered from the bone-crushing jaws of hungry Lions. His destruction was imminent; the plan was presumed flawless. But the Enemy didn't take into account Daniel's Faith in God. Daniel was a man who knew the worth of Prayer. Daniel's Faith transcended the Physical Realm and threat of danger, and delivered him from the power of the Evil Spirits using the Human Satraps who got Daniel thrown the lion's den.

The schemes of the ruling spirits manipulated King Darius and his Satraps. But God delivered Daniel from the obvious danger and the invisible attack. In fact, it was King Darius who praised God for Daniel's miraculous Deliverance!

The King realized how he allowed his Officials to manipulate him into implementing a Law that he couldn't rescind, a Law directed towards killing Daniel, one of his top Officials.

Through this event, King Darius came to Believe in Daniel's God. He proclaimed in Faith: "He delivers and rescues". The Enemy came in but was swept away by the life-changing Flood of the Spirit of God, and a Man of God who stood Faith.

The Prophet Joel wrote: "and it shall come to pass, that whosoever shall call upon the Name of the Lord shall be Delivered (Joel 2:32). While the Apostle Paul wrote: "for whosoever shall call upon the Name of the Lord shall be Saved" (Romans 10:13). We discover that Deliverance was available before Salvation was; yet Salvation, the New Birth includes Sanctification and it's offshoot, Deliverance; and yet both are the Ministry of the Holy Spirit.

*In Christ* we deal with Satan in a different way than the Old Testament. Jesus proclaimed in the synagogue, "the Spirit of the Lord is upon Me, because he has Anointed Me to Preach the Gospel to the poor; he has sent Me to Heal the brokenhearted, to Preach *Deliverance* to the Captives, and recovering of sight to the blind, to set at liberty them that are bruised, to Preach the Acceptable Year of the Lord" (Luke 4:18,19).

It was the Spirit of the Lord, the Holy Spirit that was upon the Man named Jesus of Nazareth. The Anointing empowered Jesus to preach and do the Father's will. The Christ within Jesus, the Kingdom of God, cast out and eradicated everything contrary to His nature: Bondages, Sicknesses, Diseases Poverty and Death were challenged by Jesus and He claimed the victory over them.

It wasn't who Jesus was as a Human Being that made the difference. Certainly, it was the Anointing that brought the victory, the awesome Presence of the Kingdom of God and the might behind Jehovah-Elohim rushed upon the scene.

"When the Evening was come, they brought unto Him many that were *possessed with devils*: And He cast out the spirits with His Word, and Healed all that were sick: that it might be fulfilled which was spoken by Isaiah the Prophet, saying, *Himself* took our Infirmities, and bare our Sicknesses" (Matthew 8:16, 17).

The Scriptures point out the Deliverance work of the Lord was foretold centuries earlier. He fulfilled the Will of God by Himself taking our Infirmities, Sicknesses and Diseases.

Yet that wasn't the end of the prophesies: *Himself* doesn't only mean Jesus of Nazareth ministering on Earth for three years, but ministering forever as Messiah, the High Priest of Heaven.

Even in Modern times, people testified that Jesus, *Himself,* came to their bedside and healed them; or in a life-or-death situation, Jesus appeared and Delivered them to safety.

Therefore, when the Anointing is upon us, it's the Spirit of Lord Jesus Christ (the Holy Spirit) ministering--casting out Sicknesses and Diseases.

Because the Anointing is Christ, we shouldn't accept credit for the Miracles performed through us. We humble ourselves and strive to become Obedient unto death as was Jesus. As Abraham had no confidence in the flesh neither do we.

"And when He had called unto Him His Twelve Disciples, He gave them Power against Unclean Spirits, to cast them out, and to heal all manner of Sickness and all manner of Diseases" (Matthew 10:1). This was still *Himself* working in Creation.

The Disciples were only His instruments. The Power they received was the Holy Spirit; it was Delegated Authority to minister under the same Covenant Jesus ministered under.

Jesus hadn't yet gone to the Cross so the Disciples weren't Born Again. They weren't indwelled by the Holy Spirit but understood the principles of Faith which activated the Authority of the Abrahamic Covenant, and the Name of Jehovah-Elohim.

Jesus ministered through the Legal Document known as the Abrahamic Covenant. This was His Authority to minister with and through the Holy Spirit in Creation.

As stated previously, Adam forfeited the legal possession of Creation to Satan, and God reverted to a spiritual "loophole" to maintain Fellowship with Man: A Covenant based on Faith, a Spiritual Law provided the avenue for His Spirit to work through those who willfully exercised Faith *In Him* and His Word.

God made a Faith-Oriented Covenant with Abraham. Thereafter, Faith-Oriented Miracles could be performed in Creation.

So because the New Testament Covenant wasn't yet in effect, Jesus gave the Disciples Authority similar to the Old Testament Judges, Prophets, Priests and Kings (Israel's Kings had a Leadership Anointing which they seldom used correctly), the Holy Spirit was "upon" them for Service; whereas, Salvation is the Holy Spirit "within," and the *Baptism in the Holy Spirit* "in and upon" bone-deep and like a Cloak or Mantle.

Toward the completion of Jesus' three years, He gave His Disciples the Power and Authority over Unclean Spirits. According to Jesus, Unclean Spirits were responsible for many of the Sicknesses and Diseases. He told the Disciples to *Bind* them on Earth and He through the Holy Spirit would make it so in Heavens where the Principalities and Evil Spirits congregated to control humanity.

Jesus would *Bind* the Evil Spirits ONLY in accordance to the Evil Spirits being FIRST *Bound* on the Earth. This was because the Will of Man must be involved in the warfare against Unclean Spirits. God cannot and will not interfere in our lives without our permission; and God has done all He's going to do concerning these spirits--He triumphed over them by the Cross.

"That through Death [and the Resurrection that followed] He might destroy him that had the Power over Death, that is, the Devil" (Hebrews 2:14). He abolished the Devil's Authority over the Children of God (The un-Saved are still in the Devil's Family.), and the sting of Death that is directly related to Sin, the Fall of Adam in the Garden of Eden.

He gave the Church Members Authority to Heal and Cast out Demons (But the majority of Pastors don't use their Authority, no Deliverance Services or weekly Prayer Lines; but have a "Prayer List" in a Bulletin!)

The Prayer of Agreement was another secret that Jesus revealed. "If two of you shall agree..." will manifest the Third: *Himself,* bringing the Corporate Anointing that is upon the entire Church.

Every Born Again Christian in the Body of Christ is Anointed; however, a greater Anointing exist when two or more persons are in Agreement in Prayer. This extra Anointing is the Trinity Presence in a grander Measure to manifest the agreed upon Prayer, thus being gathered together in Jesus' Name.

> Mark 11:22-24 (KJV)
> 22 "And Jesus answering said unto them, have Faith in God. 23 For verily I *say* unto you, That whosoever shall

*say* unto this mountain [Demon, Sickness, Situation) be you removed, and be you cast into the sea; and shall not doubt in his heart, but shall believe that those things which he *says* shall come to pass; he shall have whatsoever he *says.*"

Jesus gave the Disciples and all Believers the keys to the Kingdom of God. He said, "Have Faith in God". He was also stating, have the *Faith of God.*

God has tremendous Faith; if He had no Faith He couldn't create a thing! There would be no Heaven, Creation or creatures unless God had and exercised His Faith. Therefore, Faith is the Creative Principle. God has Faith in His Word----that what He says will manifest; we must also have Faith in God's Word in order to manifest the things we desire in our lives, and to ward-off the things we don't want in our lives.

To "say it" is to exercise Faith and exert the Human Will-- "And God said" (Genesis 1:3). To speak out is to express and create in words what our mind is thinking. We can have what we say, speak into existence both good and evil things.

The Holy Spirit doesn't systematically react to our mental *wants* but searches the heart to discover what we really *need*. He prefers us to speak the Word out into Creation, Pray our Petitions aloud (those who can verbally speak). Then we must believe we have the Authority and Believe what we *say* will come to pass. Spirituality is a matter of exercising Faith!

Deliverance from harassment, Unclean Spirits was the focus of Jesus' teachings. Even Salvation is technically the Deliverance from Satan and his Walking and Talking Dead Family.

So Jesus said, "and these signs shall follow them that Believe, in My Name shall they cast out Devils" they shall speak with New Tongues" (Mark 16:17). and, "behold, I give you Power [and Authority] to tread on serpents and scorpions, and over all the Power [and Authority] of the Enemy; and nothing shall by any means hurt you" (Luke 10:19). We must cleave to the Word.

The Anointing that Jesus has we have also. He gave us the best. Luke wrote of this Anointing and what a difference the Holy Spirit made to the early Christians: "How God Anointed Jesus of Nazareth with the Holy Ghost and with Power who went about doing Good, and Healing all that were oppressed of the Devil; for God was with Him" (Acts 10:38).

The Anointing is God, and God is always interested in doing Good in our lives. He grants us the Anointing so we can become like Him, to do Good Works. Without the Holy Spirit we cannot do God's work; for His works are all supernatural and we're only natural, flesh and blood creatures who can be stopped in our tracks by Unclean Spirits.

"Neither give place to the Devil" (Ephesians 4:27) was what Paul wrote to help us in our struggle against the schemes of the Devil. We must cease to be involved in those worldly activities that attract Evil Spirits into our lives. Places where sinful acts and behaviors are prominent should be avoided.

Unnecessary and unscriptural relationships with Unsaved people must be put in check. We must be conscious of what goes on in our minds and into our mouths, information and people being introduced into our lives--even our dreams must be monitored for contents because Demons also have access to our sleeping minds; sometimes the evidence of their indwelling presence are exposed in frequent nightmares or immoral dreams. Prayer is Spiritual Warfare.

And, "Submit yourselves therefore to God. Resist the Devil, and he will flee [as though in terror, as a person would flee from a burning house] from you. Draw nigh to God, and He will draw nigh to you" (James 4:7, 8). Submission, Obedience, Faith and drawing near to God constitutes resisting the Devil. Who does he flee from? The Christ in us.

"You are of God, little Children, and have overcome them [Satan's messengers]; because greater is He that is in you, than he that is in the world" (1 John 4:4). The Greater One within us causes Demon Spirits to flee. By the Power of His Word, Demons tremble and return to the shadows where they came from. The Word, Name, and the Blood of Jesus Christ Delivers us from the Accuser.

"...for the accuser of our brethren is cast down...and we overcame him [Satan] by the Blood of the Lamb, and by the word of our Testimony..." (Revelations 12:10, 11). In the end we overcame Satan through fighting the good fight of Faith and placing our *Destiny* in the delivering hands of the Lord Jesus Christ.

## *DELIVERANCE PRAYER*

Heavenly Father, I humble myself before You in the Name of Jesus Christ. I confess my sins; I am sorry for every one of them. I accept Jesus Christ as my Lord and Savior. I am Redeemed by the Blood of Jesus and seek Deliverance.

Lord, through the Power of the Holy Spirit, cleanse me. I seek to recover my freedom, wholeness, and exercise Free Will over my Spirit, Soul, Mind, and Physical Body, free of Infirmities and influence of Unclean Spirits. I denounce Satan and his Evil Spirits; his Plans, Purposes, and Pursuits. I separate myself from him and claim refuge in the Lord Jesus Christ.

I demand in the Name of Jesus immediate release from the Demonic Spirits and influences operating in my life. In Jesus' Name, I exercise Authority over you; I bind, rebuke and cast you out in Jesus' Name.

***By FAITH***: In the Name of Jesus Christ, I declare you Unclean Spirits to be unlawfully present according to the Word of God. Depart from me you cursed spirits!

***By FAITH:*** I claim the Promise of Deliverance as written in the Word of God. The Word cleanses me from all Sin. I am a temple of the Living God; and greater is Christ within me than Satan that is in the world. I belong to Christ and Him only will I serve.

***By FAITH:*** Lord Jesus Christ I accept my Deliverance. Fill me, Lord, with Your precious Holy Spirit Bless the Name of Jesus! Amen.

# CHAPTER TEN
## THE WORLD IS NOT ENOUGH

> Matthew 16:26 (KJV)
> 26 For what is a man profited, if he *shall gain the whole world, and lose his own Soul*? Or what shall a man give in exchange for his Soul?"

The Light of Israel was slowly fading into the sunset. The day began with great anticipation and the many battles were fought with sweat, blood, strained muscles and strong backs, pushing back the enemies of God. Victory was all that mattered.

King David, a man after God's own heart was tired and his hoary head full of years. His pilgrimage in this Realm began as shepherd, giant-slayer, fugitive leader of the notorious Mighty Men, then King of Israel. He was tired but his love for God and Israel was robust.

The Lord has been the strength of his life and the purpose of his ministry as King. Now he felt prepared to go the way of his ancestors. With the end of days nearing, David had more precious time to be alone with the Lord. In the solitude of his bedchamber, he laid on his face and Worshipped, Praising Him for the blessing of such an abundant life.

The Lord said David served Him with a "perfect heart". The Lord used him to conquer many nations. But in these golden years, he enjoyed rest from all his enemies. Now it was time to pass his legacy on.

King David gave this advice to Solomon, his son by Bath-Sheba: "and you, Solomon, my son, know the Lord of your father, and serve Him with a perfect heart and with a willing Mind: for the Lord searches all hearts, and understands all the imaginations of the thoughts; if you seek Him, he will be found of you; but if you forsake Him, he will cast you off forever."

The same advice applies to us today. To know the Lord and serve Him with a perfect heart and a willing Mind is what He requires.

It's not popular to serve the Lord; people mock us. Yet when they mock us they mock God: "be not deceived; God is not mocked: for whatsoever a Man sows, that shall he also reap. For he that sows to his flesh shall of the flesh reap Corruption; but he that sows to the [Holy] Spirit shall of the [Holy] Spirit reap Life Everlasting" (Galatians 6:7,8).

David didn't want Solomon to be deceived but to seek God's face and have a personal relationship with Him. This would make it difficult for Satan to trick the young King with deceptions, whereby the Congregation of Israel would Sin.

David vividly remembered the day when Satan tricked him into numbering Israel's Military. The unnecessary deaths grieved him even unto this day. He didn't want Solomon to stumble blindly into such a snare. David advised his son to learn God's Commandments and His statues, to learn the Will of God and then put that knowledge into practice. "Don't bite the hand of God that feeds you!"

Even so, David didn't pretend to be an angel but he did well in keeping himself and Israel from whoring after false gods, cults and Demonic Practices, the traditions of Demons.

King David told Solomon about his failures and successes; if he hadn't told Solomon someone else would've told him. David arranged the Murder of Bath-Sheba's former Husband, Uriah, one of David's Mighty Men. He did this to hide his *adulterous affair*.

King David had Intercourse with Bath-Sheba while Uriah was at battle (2 Samuel 11:26,27). She became pregnant.

God forgave David--but the point of the discussion was to impart wisdom and understanding of the nature of the flesh, and the enemies of God who would take advantage of Solomon and his great position as King of Israel. Solomon being faithful to God would enable God to strengthen him and beat back His enemy, the Devil.

Israel's perseverance and prosperity was in King Solomon's hands. And the heart of the King of Israel was known to God, even the imaginations of his heart!

Israel was God's chosen nation to bring forth the Messiah. No other nation received so much of God's attention and attacks by Satan than Israel. This was because the other nations had already accepted Cain's religion and demonic slavery; but Israel had Divine Destiny.

> 2 Chronicles 1:7, 10 (KJV)
> 7 "In that night did God appear unto Solomon, and said unto him, Ask what I shall give thee. 10 Give me now Wisdom and Knowledge..."

Solomon discovered that after years of preparing lead Israel, when the time came to rule, he was unprepared; he lacked Wisdom and Knowledge. He remembered what his father David told him: Wisdom and knowledge came from God. Solomon petitioned God and received an answer that night.

It wasn't unusual for God to receive petitions from people requesting help. Many of the requests were honorable, others were selfish: Riches, fame, revenge...but Solomon didn't ask for these mundane trophies, but asked for Divine Wisdom and Knowledge to rule according to the Word of God.

God was pleased with his request and granted it. God also gave him wealth and fame far exceeding the past and future Kings throughout the Earth. Solomon became the most influential man in the world.

Immediately, Solomon went to work building the Nation of Israel. He purchased and assembled hundreds of chariots and horsemen. He sent to foreign lands and purchased building materials and hired tradesmen to build the Temple for the Name of the Lord and his own Palace.

Solomon also established a Navy at Tarshish and Shipyards for his Commercial Trade Routes his merchants traded all over the known world. Kings brought gifts of Gold, Silver, Gemstones, Ivory, Spices and Exotic Animals for his Zoo (1 Kings 10:14-22).

Many of the Kings gave their daughters to Solomon and he married them.

King Solomon assembled a work force of skilled and unskilled workers, raised the taxes and foreign tributes to build the spectacular Temple of the Lord, roads and other projects.

In the Temple and the King's Palace, were gold and silver vessels, shields and candlesticks of beaten gold. Solomon's Temple and Palace had the best singers, musicians, servants, cupbearers and magnificent Royal Apparel.

Solomon possessed Wisdom and Knowledge to speak and write about Heaven, Earth, Ocean and Sky; Solomon knew more than others everything worth knowing.

> 1 Kings 11:1,3 (KJV)
> 1 "But King Solomon loved many strange woman… 3 And he had Seven Hundred Wives, Princesses, and Three Hundred Concubines: and his wives turned away his heart."

Solomon gained the whole world. He lived in splendor and material bliss. Whatever his heart desired was immediately brought to him. When foreign nations desired peace and Commerce with Israel that King gave Solomon one or more of their daughters.

Solomon now had a Palace full of young women. The problem with this arrangement, God was against it.

Satan knew Solomon's weakness, his lust of the flesh; so Satan provided the objects tailor made for Solomon's destruction.

Before long the heathen women had Solomon building temples of worship to their native gods. These became the notorious High Places. The woman, grossly outnumbered him, overpowered his senses with their sensuality, sexuality, charm and perfumed bodies; they slowly coerced Solomon to burn a little incense, chants a little, an occasional sacrifice and dance.

Before long, Solomon and Israel continuously burned incense, offered regular sacrifices, participated in the Orgies with the Cult Prostitutes (who prostituted for the temple high places) and worshipped entirely the Dark Side of reality.

They forsook the Temple where the Name of the Lord was. "And the Lord was angry with Solomon, because his heart was turned from the Lord God of Israel, which had appeared unto him twice" (1 Kings 11:9).

The Lord appeared to Solomon twice; these strange gods never appeared to Solomon once. His infatuation with the things of the Demonic Realm and desiring to satisfy his manipulative women-- annulled the Anointing of Great Wisdom and Knowledge God gave him. Solomon was far wiser and intelligent than all his women put together!

Unfortunately, Solomon underestimated the cunning of Satan; those Kings gave their daughters to Solomon to acquire favor, influence and bring down the mighty Solomon. Those foreign Kings didn't like him; they hated his guts! Exploited as they were, they in turn exploited---offered their daughters as a sacrifice--- to bring down the most powerful King and Nation on earth.

The Evil Prince Spirits behind the thrones of the nations knew Solomon had a Sexual Addiction; his flesh yearned for pleasure. Then the foreign Kings, mere servants of the Prince Spirits behind the veil, offered Solomon their daughters, who in turn practiced witchcraft on Solomon; and his wives lured King Solomon away from the Lord God of Israel.

Unless the Lord was removed from the heart of Solomon, Satan couldn't capture the Throne of Israel; and it was indeed a trophy!

God made Solomon wealthy. The wealth Solomon possessed had no mind of its own, but could be used for the education and economical advancement of Israel. It was also God's intent for the Temple and King's Palace be exquisite, that Solomon's dynasty be spectacular and glorious to all the nations, his Wisdom and Knowledge envious to the end of the earth.

Many of the projects Solomon completed were of secular benefit to Israel and the world. It was when he realized that he could have whatever he wanted---even the entire world, was when he started the downward spiral. Solomon became mesmerized over women, extravert living, power, prestige, glamour and praise of men, coupled with the desire to please people more than pleasing God.

God's desires that we have material prosperity and blessings. He wants our store to remain full. The wealth we obtain must always be a tool used for the good of Humanity and for His Glory. We cannot afford to be stingy and selfish.

Today at the top of the financial pyramid are multi-billionaires, billionaires and multi-millionaires; below them are millionaires and everybody else. A minority of people own the Businesses, Real Estate and other profit-making organizations.

When we believe the flattery, the back-slapping publicity and consider ourselves a law unto ourselves—a King Solomon--and measure ourselves by ourselves, we're heading for a fall.

Jesus Christ is the Standard for righteous and moral behavior. He is not to be mocked.

"For we brought nothing into this world, and it is certain we can carry nothing out. But they that will be rich fall into temptation and a snare [of Satan], and many foolish and hurtful lusts, which drown men in Destruction and Prediction. for the *love of money* is the root of all evil; which some coveted after, they erred from the Faith, and pierced themselves through with many sorrows" (1 Timothy 6:7,9,10).

The New Testament Scriptures are the Testimony of the Old Testament examples. The Temple was beautiful and sacred then and the Human Temple where the Anointing dwells is supposed to be beautiful and sacred now; what corrupted humanity in ancient times is still around, pressing to snare, corrupt, drown us in many foolish and hurtful lust.

>Ecclesiastes 1:14 (KJV)
>14 "I have seen all the works that are done under the sun;

and behold, all is vanity and vexation of spirit.

Solomon, later in life, the Preacher was King of Israel. He had everything he wanted in life but wasn't content with his life. Deep within was a longing for something that his wealth, women or fame couldn't get him. His Soul longed for an inner tranquility.

In response to this longing Solomon dispatched convoys across the ocean and around the world in hopes his merchants would discover something new and bring it back.

Then he realized there was nothing new under the sun (Ecclesiastes 1:9). His Soul's desire to be comforted in the flesh was in vain. The emptiness inside made his words echo in his chest. Several times he conspired to rob himself of the loneliness; the emptiness and futility no longer would be satisfied Sexual Intercourse, trophies, worldly trivia, or treasures of the world.

Finally, he realized it was all vanity, an well-orchestrated illusion—he spent his life chasing the wind! And he knew that the immortal words of his father David were true--that God alone was his portion and the strength of his life.

Therefore Solomon put to ink his revelations. When he looked back over his life, reflected upon l the years of his Reign, he was disappointed. He pondered how Man spent their lives laboring under the sun, hoarding materiality and sensual pleasures.

Solomon wasn't a pessimist, in fact he loved life. He only regretted wasting so much of his and seeing others do the same.

Solomon wasn't disgruntled, angry or blaming God for his misery; he only concluded the obvious--what he discovered in his fool life, what others before and after him discovered by living a wasteful life without God. Everything he accomplished reeked of vanity; it was useless, foolish, an exercise in futility.

When Solomon became the wisest man on Earth, the Kings and Queens of foreign countries--including the Queen of Sheba came to Jerusalem to learn from him. He researched and taught hundreds of subjects. He displayed Divine Wisdom to judge and wrote many pieces of literature: Ecclesiastes, Song of Solomon, several Psalms and other works. With all his practical insights on life he failed to take his own advice.

Now he bowed in Humility and Repentance, for leaving God out of his life for so many years---and leading Israel down the path of futility and Darkness.

Solomon purposed in his heart to warn future generations to avoid the evil "vexation of spirit" and bitterness, of bumping our head against the stone wall of error, and living a meaningless existence apart from God. Through trials and tribulations Solomon became the voice of experience. He resigned to Believe: "Let us hear the conclusion of the whole matter: Fear (Reverence] God, and keep His Commandments; for *this is the whole duty of Man*" (Ecclesiastes 12:13).

The searching for peace and joy has driven Man to despair. True happiness can't be found in Human Relationship or material things; because when Spirits of Greed or Lust is in control of our lives it won't be satisfied no matter how much material wealth or sexual conquest are had.

"The leach has two daughters, crying, Give! Give! (Proverbs 30:15). Through circumstances beyond our control material possessions can be lost and if we're depending on them for support, we'll collapse also.

Our life-long search should be to know the Lord Jesus Christ better. He gives Wisdom, Knowledge and the Fruit of the Spirit to all who diligently seek Him. He is the Restorer of our Souls and leads us in the Path of Righteousness for His Name's Sake (Psalms 23:3).

We befriend the emptiness of vacuum Space when we befriend materiality. The love of money, wealth is a false companion and a merciless taskmaster. The hut for wealth and fame has driven many well-intentioned people into Depression, Criminal Activity, unnecessary personal and financial risks.

Consider how many people have lost their lives due to the love of money? The insatiable longing for riches becomes a consuming fire. It devours the Mental Energy of the Soul, leaves it shipwrecked, and burned out.

Nevertheless, the cure for the bottomless pit of emptiness is the centering of our Mind and soul upon our Destiny with Jesus Christ. He fills the emptiness, the longing for Internal Companionship, company for the Human Spirit. We must fill our lives with the Holy Spirit, serving God and not ourselves or the world. The key therefore is to seek first the Kingdom of God and all our other needs will be automatically met.

Solomon's purpose for writing Ecclesiastes was to shake our confidence from trusting in our *tainted* Human Nature to satisfy ourselves. We can't satisfy ourselves because the flesh is never satisfied, always controlling, bossy, a miserable creature of impulses, habits, feelings, a self-gratifying animal.

This wisdom comes from the Throne of God; all works done under the sun in the flesh are futile, vanity and vexation of the Holy Spirit. Only assignments given to us by God are worth anything in Eternal Weight of Glory.

We must always ask the Holy Spirit to search us and examine our motives behind what we do. Our self-examinations often deceives us; we see what we want to see. God will inform us when He has work to do through us. And whatever it is must be done for His Glory and not ours.

The certainty of physical death and the Iniquity associated with being Human makes all Human efforts futile. Whatever we accumulate in life we'll leave behind. We came into this world with nothing and materially we'll leave out with the same--yet we can leave with Salvation.

We'll leave material goods on this side of the grave and Salvation can be taken beyond; Salvation (Saved) is something that we are, not just something that we have, when we live this world.

The things that we have, materiality will be left to the care of someone else. If we work ourselves to death, there's no guarantee that our children won't spend it foolishly. Then why should we labor feverishly for these material things, when death brings a final separation from them?

Consider this: There's no time to live a selfish, stupid life! We desperately need the Vision and Wisdom that comes from above. Only the Spirit of God can deliver us from the mindless, medieval drive for riches, fame and acceptance. Only God can spare us the Rat Race and grant hope beyond a reasonable doubt.

Death doesn't have to have the last laugh; we can laugh in its face. Sometimes we are envious when we consider the prosperity of the wicked, even the lifestyles of the rich and famous.

The *love* of fame and fortune is contrary to righteousness. All the material things in the world, is not enough values for one Human Soul. Spirits of Greed often attract themselves to even the average Time Clock Workers, Entertainers, Athletics and Career Professionals alike.

If we're not rooted and grounded in the Word of God, we may find ourselves slaving in the salt mines of Iniquity only to purchase more "stuff"; being compelled by the fire of greed (not wise investing) to purchase more property, mansions to keep up with the Obama's, a bigger slice of the American Pie. And of course, no mansion is complete without servants and expensive cars. Our luxury spirit demands satisfaction until we're buying solely for the *love* of it, keeping up the image of who we're "supposed" to be in the Tabloids or Public Opinion.

We discover that we're a *have-not* by looking at what others *have*. Surely we purpose in our hearts to surpass others at any cost to prove that we're more intelligent and resourceful.

Perhaps the desire to succeed becomes an obsession, a balancing act between Credit Card Companies, Retail Stores and other notable Creditors.

As a results we spend most of our waking hours manipulating people over the telephone. Outside the home we scheme our way into the higher echelon of society to acquire a more prestigious position with greater financial rewards, even sleeping with Executives to move up higher---to purchase more stuff.

We crave respect and attention from those around us and choose our "associates" by their Net Worth. God, if He was ever in our lives has long been given a back seat to the advancement in the world. We are drowning to the cesspool of materiality; for the *love of money* has gotten us in its grip. We aren't happy; the more money we get the more trouble it brings. One thing for certain we found that money can't buy happiness or true love.

Money can buy a house but not a home, sex but not real love; and money can't buy a ticket to Heaven:

Many believe that Fame and Fortune is their *Destiny,* as though it is the *End Game*, the ultimate goal; perhaps Fame and Fortune is within our Destiny, but it shouldn't be all there is!

For example: The world of glamour, movie industry and professional sports, society lifts many of these personalities up as Latter Day gods and goddesses. The "beautiful people" are envied and secretly worshipped and given huge amounts of money to "rule" the Airwaves.

At the end of each year they're nominated for various awards according to their contribution to Humanity--given plaques or statues. Many live for the day they receive one of these gods--or rather, a *status symbol* that makes them a god in their own eyes and the eyes of their fans. If we live solely for image sake than we're missing the meaning of life---just like King Solomon did.

In our profession what do we really contribute to Humanity that lifts the spiritual and moral consciousness? Or are we simply watering the Tree of Knowledge of Good and Evil so it will survive another year?

Multi-million dollar sports and entertainment deals are common but there's never enough money for Homeless Shelters, Senior Citizen Care, Rehabilitation Centers or Public Schools. Ironically, Prison Guards make more money than School Teachers--is there a connection here?

Billions are spent on Space Exploration, (If an alien civilization out there is living in Peace, they need to stay away from Earth!) Endangered Species, Fashion, Cosmetics and Entertainment of all sorts, but on the whole the Human Race remains morally bankrupt, sick, depraved and indifferent towards God.

God said, "The heart is deceitful above all things, desperately wicked; who can know it?" (Jeremiah 17:9).

We have the technology to travel into Outer Space, destroy enire cities and laws to lock up our children--but our priorities are wrong; we use our wisdom, knowledge, strength and wealth for the wrong things. If we use them for the glory of God we'll accomplish more, lift the spiritual and moral consciousness of Man to greater heights. We must push aside what was previously accepted as normal Human *Destiny*, goals and subsequent behaviors.

> Psalms 37:1,2, (KJV)
> 1 "Fret not yourself because of evildoers, neither be envious against the workers of Iniquity.2 For they shall soon be cut down like the grass..."

We are but grass and God is the lawnmower. Christians and non-Christians are equally warned not to be material minded and commit crimes against God and Society for the sake of money, whereby selling-out to the world instead of the Living Christ. The "wicked" are those who defy heaven and Earth in order to T*raffic Iniquity*. Humanity must count the cost.

We all know people operating outside of the law. We know their lifestyles, perhaps our own family members are involved in illegal transactions and *Trafficking Iniquity*.

King David said he saw the wicked (or group of wicked people) in Great Authority, seemly invincible—turning their noses up at the law of God--but one day the scales tipped, sought True Balance and they paid the price!

They departed; David considered their lifestyle, mortal determination to live forever, but couldn't sustain it; David went by the place they used to live. He couldn't find any trace of them or their accomplishments. David searched diligently for them but still couldn't find them. God cut them off from the Earth Realm.

It seemed like they were untouchable, Teflon People while alive; but God reached out and touched them, and they withered like the grass of the field. There is a lesson to be learned: Although a Criminal may es-cape the Criminal Justice System by means of flight, bribery, witness tampering or witness intimidation---they won't escape out of God's hand in this life or the Hereafter.

> Hebrews 1:5 (NIV)
> 5 "Keep your lives from the love of money and be content with what you have, because God has said, never will I leave you; never will I forsake you."

Again, this message resounds. It was written to the Early Church Members who obviously needed to hear this; and so, in this area, people have not changed.

God made King Solomon rich; but no so he could flaunt it, or use it the way he did (building the heathen High Places etc.) Many are focused on riches and not on Jesus Christ. It's equally wrong to love, trust and be proud because of our riches or popularity, but use these blessings to ease Human suffering.

Being content with what we have doesn't mean we must stay at a certain level in society and not seek advancement. It means to always be thankful and appreciative to God, acknowledging the indwelling Christ as being eternally PRICELESS, our help to obtain riches; with our hope and trust always in the Lord to effect at His Will and Timing any promotions, giving thanks and credit to Him when it comes.

Then when we arrive at the top of our field --and perhaps an award, Super Bowl Ring, interview or generous financial Contract is presented to us--PUBLICLY GIVE GOD THE PRAISE AND GLORY for enabling and strengthening us.

We're not to envy the financial tyrants or be Scrooges to our neighbors. Otherwise our feet will be in slippery places and one day we'll fall and can't get up. So what does it profit us to gain the world and lose our souls? ***The world is not enough!***

# CHAPTER ELEVEN
## JEHOVAH-TSKENU

For over Three Years the Sanhedrin Council, the Jewish Supreme Court sent investigators to gather enough evidence against Jesus to Indict and bring Him to Trial. Jehovah-Tskenu, the Lord our Righteousness preached messages of Repentance, Faith and the New Birth and had turned the world upside down (Acts 17:6). Everyone was talking about Jesus of Nazareth as He preached the Word of Faith (Romans 10:8).

His Miracles were awesome; and so they wanted to kill him because of them. Nevertheless Jesus boldly went forth teaching the Principles of the Kingdom of God. He revealed to his audience how much God loved and affectionately cared for them. He Delivered them from Sickness, Oppression and the usual slavery of the Devil. Jesus made God a real Person to them!

The Religious Authority believed they had no need for His brand of Righteousness. They had Abraham, Moses and the Prophets to stand before God in their behalf. Not only that, their righteousness came by the Mosaic Law; it provided the right relationship needed to enter the Pearly Gates.

The Religious Leaders believed they fulfilled all the requirements of the Law and they were proud of their humility! As far as they were concerned, Jesus was a rebel, a Dissident, hadn't attained their social and political circle; Jesus had no scholarly credentials or references—no Theological Degree.

Therefore, they would go to the grave in defiance of His Teachings---even if they were correct. How dare this nobody---this carpenter's son from Nazareth, a mortal man with no religious affiliation, claim to be the Son of God! And what a tale He told when He said He came down from Heaven --when we know His father Joseph and Mary His mother! This man attempts to pervert the, the Judean Religion with the blasphemes of a Gentile-lovers schemes!

The major reason why Jesus spoke against the Sanhedrin Council wasn't because they feverishly tried to kill Him and destroy His ministry--though in itself was a good reason--but because they were hypocrites and led others astray.

The Righteousness the Jews claimed to trust in they didn't have. They didn't understand the Mosaic Law, the Law of Sin and Death was becoming obsolete as the New Testament Covenant with Jesus Christ as its High Priest rapidly approached.

Jesus told His audience their Righteousness must exceed, be authentic, tangible, able to withstand the test of time and Eternity, a Righteousness that comes from God and not from Man. If they didn't possess this Righteousness they would miss the Kingdom.

But Jesus assured them that through Faith the prostitutes, publicans and sinners would enter into the Kingdom before the so-called religious people and their beloved Law. To that the poor and downhearted sinners took courage, believed in His Word and followed Him wherever He went. He was the Great Teacher and Physician and they were His students and patients.

Often Jesus was verbally abused because He was with sinners. Jesus practiced the *Separation* of Himself from the thoughts and acts of Sin, not *Segregation* from sinners who needed Him most.

The Pharisees believed they would be Defiled, become Ceremoniously Unclean by touching what they considered contaminated things. They especially believed that a Righteous Jew shouldn't touch or be touched by a sinner, especially the Gentiles; and never enter the home of a Gentile, or let them into their own home, or eat with them.

But Jesus deflated their Theology by declaring His mission: A secular Physician treats the sick and must occasionally touch to examine the patients. The Divine Physician, Himself, didn't come to treat the healthy, the Righteous (though there were none but He) but bring sinners to Repentance!

In Matthew Chapter 23 are the Seven Woes:

"***Woe unto you*** Scribes, Pharisees, Hypocrites! These were Jesus' warning to the Spiritual Leaders of his day and ours. These

Leaders propagate unrighteous doctrines whereby excluding themselves from entering the Kingdom of Heaven, and become stumbling blocks to others, keeping them also from entering Heaven. Their long prayers sound righteous, their words seem sincere. But in reality it's phony, crowd-pleasing drama.

***"Woe unto you*** Scribes and Pharisees, Hypocrites!" This woe gave Jesus because of the great efforts expended by the false teachers spreading anti-Christ Doctrines to persuade us to substitute God's Word, the Bible for other so-called "inspired" writings. These Spiritual Leaders attempt to annul the wonderful righteousness that Christ wants to perfect in us. These lost Souls steal God's Glory and the Inheritance promised to His lost sheep. They can make us more a Child of Hell than we were before we got Saved.

These Leaders promote themselves, the conclusions of their minds, man-made traditions, rituals and Mind Control tactics to keep us in line. They tell us if we go to another Church we would be condemned. These Leaders don't want us to think and use our Free Will. These Leaders "say and do not." They bind us with heavy burdens, grievous to bear, lay them on our shoulders and walk away; they pressure us to do useless, futile labor under the sun, works that God hasn't ordained. These works make the Leader's ministry (not Christ's) look prosperous.

"***Woe unto you, blind guides***..." When a Spiritual Leader has no Spiritual Vision, his people perish! He must have God's Priorities, Biblically sound or there's confusion. The guide cannot be blind because the blind cannot lead the blind; they will both fall into the hands of Satan and the Pit of Hell.

The gift cannot be greater than the altar of God, the Giver; and our Material Gifts cannot be greater in value than we are. For this would be the *love of money*. Because a Church Leader is paid a large salary, is on TBN or another Christian Channel, has a large Designer Church and thousands in attendance, doesn't mean his Teaching and Preaching is accurate: He may be a Blind Guide; whereas, a Church Leader receiving a lesser salary, has a smaller church building and Congregation, may preach the Truth, with

Miracles, Signs and Wonders following.

If a Leader gets his reward here what will be left to receive later? The financial rewards, expensive cars, clothes, home, lavish hotel accommodations when traveling, and the chief seats at Conferences; plus the titles Reverend, Pastor, Arch-Bishop, Bishop or Apostle--- should not blind the eyes of the servant of God. The greatest Preachers and in the Body of Christ are only servants!

"***Woe to you, Scribes and Pharisees, Hypocrites***!" Let's not get materialistic or beside ourselves to think tithes or wealth are purchasing our ticket to Heaven. Grace has nothing to do with having the bigger tithe, neither is it a measuring rod for Spirituality or favor with God.

Money must be kept silent and in its place. If it decides to "talk" we should not listen. We're the ones who talk and use money, not the other way around. Neither should we preach mostly "Give Us More Money Sermons", and ignore the heavier things such as Repentance, Faith, Salvation, Deliverance, Healing, Justice, Mercy and Love; the Fruit of the Spirit should always be top priority.

The proverbial "strain at a Nat and swallow a camel" should not apply to Christians. God's concerns should be our concerns.

The Righteous Church of Jesus Christ is concerned with the *Adoption of Children* by Jesus Christ (Children who will later become Mature, Revealed, as the Sons of God.); the tithes and offerings don't take precedence to the divine mission.

Tithes and offerings are an outward expression of Obedience, Faith and Worship, through giving towards the Great Commission. We make Disciples by witnessing and assisting in the advancement of the Kingdom of God and the preparation of the Saints.

"***Woe unto you Scribes and Pharisees, Hypocrites***! God wants us to look good on the inside and outside too. For this cause has the Holy Spirit of God indwelled us. His Presence radiates from the center of our being to the outer circumference.

Many religious leaders---including Christian Leaders and their disciples are like the Scribes and Pharisees---look and sound good on the outside, but like a cup, sparkling clean on the outside, but inside full of filth, corruption, not fitting to serve anyone. Jesus said the *inside* must be cleansed then the cup is really clean and fit to be in service.

The Scriptures warn us about perpetrating a fraudulent (fake) spirituality before the Congregation of the Lord and the World. Our private worlds at home, work and leisure time activities should also reflect Who we claim to be. We can't get away with leading a sinful private life.

And we must give our spouse, children, neighbors and coworkers with Genuine Love. They will see our good works and glorify our Father in Heaven.

It would be easier to witness to love ones and coworkers if we're a incandescent lighthouse upon a hill overlooking the dark and stormy sea. Many will come to the Shore we represent to find safety and total peace.

**"*Woe unto you, Scribes and Pharisees, Hypocrites!*"** Again Jesus compared the Religious Leaders and their disciples as great pretenders. He declared with all honesty they appeared as white sepulchers--beautiful, artistic, solid and outwardly clean--but within are full of dead people's rotting flesh and bones, uncleanness and despair. The contents of the sepulcher also represents the dead world and those who fall in love with it.

We can't allow ourselves to become like those white sepulchers. Neither should we allow ourselves to be packed with the death of the world, the Hypocrisy and Iniquity. Pretending to be spiritual to cover up the need for Deliverance; so hiding our sins isn't the answer; One day our sins will tell on us!

Jesus Christ provided Deliverance for His Saints of the Local Churches. Badly needing Deliverance, we try to bluff our way into people's lives under the guise of Christianity.

"***Woe unto you, Scribes and Pharisees, Hypocrites!*** The Scribes and Pharisees hated Jesus! He publicly uncovered them and exposed their moral nudity and sent them searching for fig leaves!

Jesus called them Hypocrite, Fools, Blind Guides, Vipers and other descriptive names. This last *woe* was given because they pretended to diligently seek Wisdom and Knowledge of the Law, and embraced with Genuine Love the sayings of the Prophets-- whom their forefathers mercilessly killed! Now the present Sanhedrin Council plotted to kill Him as well. Jesus told them they hadn't learned a thing.

The Jewish Elders financed the construction of the Tombs of the Prophets. A Prophet of God couldn't die outside of Israel; seldom did a Prophet die of old age either!

"You Serpents, you Generation of Vipers, how can you escape the damnation of Hell?" (Matthew 23:33). Jesus convicted them of following in their ancestor's footsteps. Their history was violent, bloody and rebellious to every principle God stood for.

As Christians, we're not to follow in our ancestor's evil ways but to put on the Righteousness of Christ. The Old Man has passed away--his funeral was the day we got Saved--now we're New Creatures with the Breastplate of Righteousness protecting our head from the whispers of Satan.

Satan, an ancient enemy, constantly provoked Israel to Murder the Messengers of God, isn't our Spiritual Leader anymore. We shall not allow Satan to make our homes desolate. Now we proclaim from the rooftops: "Blessed is He that cometh in the Name of the Lord." The Spirit of God bears witness with our Human Spirit that we're the Children of God.

> Isaiah 64:6  Zachariah 3:1,3,4
> 6 But we are all as an Unclean Thing, and all our [self] righteousness are as filthy rags; and we all do fade as a leaf; and our Iniquities, like the wind, have taken us away. 1 And he showed me Joshua the High Priest standing before the Angel of the Lord, and Satan standing at his right hand to resist him. 3 Now Joshua was clothed with filthy garments...4 ...take away the filthy garments from him... and I will clothe you with change of raiment."

Isaiah proclaimed the Word of the Lord concerning the reason Israel suffered so many hardships. Isaiah proclaimed to Israel God's Judgment and His Loving Kindness. God warned them that from the beginning of Creation Man refused to listen to Him and their eyes haven't seen the treasures He had for them.

By substituting their own righteousness for God's Righteousness angered Him. They sinned and Trafficked Iniquity everyplace Man laid his head.. Yet in the end, God would save His Prize Creation called Man.

Isaiah proclaimed the Gospel to his rebellious neighbors: "All our righteousness are as filthy rags"--worthless, contaminated, soiled rags--good only for the fire.

Centuries we've been passing off these filthy rags to one another and to God. But though we readily accept one another's self-righteousness, God won't accept it. It was God's Righteousness that gave Life and Health to the dry Jewish bones.

The Lord showed Zachariah the same thing. Joshua, the first High Priest under Moses' Administration stood before the Angel of the Lord, Jesus Christ. Satan was present to accuse Joshua. The accusation was true in that Joshua had sin in his life. His righteousness was draped around him as filthy rags. But the Lord rebuked Satan because it was the Lord who chose "imperfect" Joshua and Israel to represent Him in Creation. Joshua was a stick snatched from the fire of sin and made useful to the Lord's plans.

Jesus ordered the self-righteous rags removed and His Imputed Righteousness based upon Joshua's Faith---new clean garments---placed upon Joshua. His sins were now covered.

Satan continues to accuse the Saints before the Throne of God. His accusations are based on our sinful lifestyles and conformity to his world and the Law of Sin and Death.

Yet the Lord said, "I will cloth you with a change of raiment [righteousness]." And put a miter, a golden crown upon our heads; and with His righteousness we can walk in His ways and govern the house of the Lord. We will be a people "wondered at", a people crucified with Him, redeemed and resurrected, whose robes have been washed in the Blood of the Lamb.

> Galatians. 2:20 (KJV)
> 20 "I am crucified with Christ: nevertheless I live; yet not I, but Christ lives in me; and the life which I now live in the flesh I live by the Faith of the Son of God, who loved me, and gave Himself for me"

The I am Crucified with Christ-Faith and Righteousness changed us. "For He has made Him to be Sin for us, who knew no Sin; that we might be made the Righteousness of God *In Him*" (2 Corinthians 5:21). We're righteous because we've been Crucified with Christ and accepted His Righteousness.

This Wonderful and *Destiny-Changing* Righteousness God predestinated into our lives was conferred upon us the moment we Repented, Confessed our Sins, Confessed Faith in Jesus Christ as our Personal Lord and Savior. Without His Righteousness, we're doomed to roam the face of the Earth, die and be lost. God says: My child, turn from your wicked ways!

The words "Righteous and Righteousness" has become synonymous to most people with God, Christ, the Holy Spirit--but not the Earthbound Church; when in fact, the Church in Heaven is Righteous, and so is the Earthbound Church.

Righteousness as it applies to Christians, is Imputed, placing us in a Right-relationship or Right-Standing with God. That relationship began when we sat down with Him and ironed out our differences, opened a line of communication. Immediately our *Friendship and Relationship* became an eternal reality recorded in the archives of Heaven.

Again, as Members of the Heavenly and Earthbound Church (In reality, there's only one Church) we're righteous because He's Righteous; it's all or nothing.

> Romans 3:22 10:10 (KJV)
> 22 "Even the Righteousness of God is by Faith of Jesus Christ unto all them that believe...Righteousness shall

reign in life by one, Jesus Christ. 10 For with the heart Man Believes unto Righteousness."

Romans 5:7 confirms that our Righteousness, like Abraham's was Imputed, counted to us as a Gift of God in response to our Faith in Jesus Christ. Righteousness doesn't come by works, being good, reading the Bible or attending Church--it's only by Faith. If good works pleased God and He granted Righteousness because of it, there was no need for Jesus to die on the Cross for our Sins.

So among the Born Again Believers, there are no degrees of Righteousness; some Christians aren't more Righteous than others. Some may be more Obedient, Disciplined, Faithful, have Miracle-working Faith, Gifted, Pray and talk to God more than others---but that doesn't make them more Righteous, since our Righteousness comes from God as a gift to all His Children.

Imputed Righteousness is the reason Jesus said, "With God all things are possible" (Matthew 19:26). Then he also stated, "...all things are possible to him that believes" (Mark 9:23).

If we believe the first verse is true we must also believe the second verse because it's written in the same Bible.

Jesus Christ imputes His Righteousness in us so we can do all things. So it's *Himself* Healing the Infirmities and ministering to the world as the Greater One within us (1 John 4:4). For it is God which works in you both to will and to do his good pleasure" (Philippians 2:13). So, how can a Righteous God be in a Christian and the Christian not be Righteous too? And sense Christians are indwelled with the ENTIRE PERSON of God the Holy Spirit---not a piece of Him---how can we not be victorious in life?

James 5:14-16

14 "Is any Sick among you? Let him call for the Elders of the Church; and let them Pray over him, anointing him with oil in the Name of the Lord: 15 And the Prayer of Faith shall save the Sick, and the Lord shall raise him up

...16 the effectual fervent Prayer of a Righteous Man avails [makes tremendous, dynamic power available] much."

Satan and religious people present misinformation and mystery concerning who is or isn't a righteous person. So many Christians don't accept the fact we're the Righteous People the Bible describes in the New Testament.

The problem is we fail to accept our privileges as the Righteous; to Commune, Fellowship with God, Pray, call on the Elders of the Church to be Anoint with oil when sickness comes. This is partly because of old traditions--that Religious Spirit operating again-- has us believing it's some twisted virtue or blessing to be sick, or our "thorn" to keep us humble.

We must not assume that we're so spiritual and have received such mind-blowing Revelations of Christ that we "require" a thorn in the side to keep us humble!

Not applying the Scriptures correctly many Christians die prematurely or live defeated, powerless lives, and thus don't enter in or fulfill their *Destiny*.

All Christian can Pray or lay hands on the Sick: ALL CHRISTIANS ARE RIGHTEOUS! Why does the Prayer of Faith work? Because it's not us but *Himself* who is the Healer, Deliverer and Provider.

A little something to ponder: Judas Iscariot, the Disciple who betrayed Jesus to the Sanhedrin and the Romans, was given Power to Heal the Sick and to cast out Unclean Spirits along with the other Eleven Disciples. There's not record showing that Judas performed any less than the other Disciples; since it was the Faith of the sick person that Healed them. If Jesus could use Judas Iscariot to heal and cast out Demons, He can use anyone.

As our pilgrimage continues our measure of Faith should increase. Faith applied to the righteousness we already have, the more victorious our Christian ministry will be. For our Imputed Righteousness by Faith *exceeds the righteousness of the Scribes, Pharisees and Hypocrites!*

# CHAPTER TWELVE
## SIT, WALK AND STAND

Ephesians 2:6 (KJV)
6 "And has raised us up together, and made us *Sit* in the heavenly places in Christ Jesus."

**Sit With Him:** We often think of Jesus Christ as God's only begotten Son who *Sits* at the Right Hand of God. It's true that Jesus is the "First" Son--but since then the Father has begotten many "Spiritual" Sons and Daughters into the Family. Jesus was the only Son *Sitting* at the throne--now the Church *Sits* with the Father also. We *Sit In Him* as people lifted from the grave to *Sit* with Christ in glory.

As Christians we've been granted a heavenly seat, a position far above the Demonic Kingdom of Ruling Spirits of the Lower Realms. As Jesus *Sits* and commands we *Sit* and command; we share His Victory and Faith to cause mountains to move.

We're blessed with every Spiritual Blessing in Heaven (Ephesians 2:3). We're Holy, Righteous, Anointed with God's Compassion and Agape Love.

In Luke 10:38-42, at first glance the Scriptures appear to record only a domestic argument: Martha wanted Jesus to referee. But Jesus took the opportunity, as with other life situations, to explain the Mysteries of the Kingdom of God.

Martha was extremely "careful and troubled about many things." She busily occupied herself with trying to please the Master with works inspired by what she thought would please Him. She wanted to show her Love by preparing a good meal. Yet Jesus never told her to be in the kitchen. He didn't say He was hungry. She became so caught up in her works she became bitter, resentful and even jealous with Mary for not sharing her enthusiasm at rattling the pots and pans!

Jesus told Martha that "one thing was needed: And Mary has chosen that good part." Choosing the "good part" is a Free Will act, to *Sit* at the feet of Christ and learn of Him; it was more important than Martha's material offering. Martha's offering was truly one of love for Jesus, emotionally flowing from her kind heart--yet to *Sit*, "be still and know that *I Am* God..." (Psalms 46:10) was of eternal weight. Jesus declared that this one thing would not be taken away from her; and neither will it be taken away us either. Yes, God has raised us up to *Sit* with Him in the heavenly places.

>Psalms 23:1-3
>1 The Lord is my Shepherd; I shall not want. 2 He makes me to lie down in green pastures. He leads me beside the still waters. 3 He Restores my Soul; He leads me in the Paths of Righteousness for His Name's Sake.

**Walk With Him**: David wrote that the Lord was his Shepherd. David spent his early years as a shepherd boy watching his father Jesse's sheep (1 Samuel 16:10). David wrote the Twenty-Third Psalms out of his own experiences; he saw a similarity in how God leads His Children.

David led and provided protection for the sheep. He knew that without a shepherd the predators would devour the sheep. Sheep have no natural defenses, mental or physical attributes to ward off a lightning-swift beast. But David was a skillful shepherd; he once killed a lion and a bear. He was willing to give his life for the sheep.

As long as the sheep obeyed David's voice they were safe. Occasionally a sheep went its own way and got lost. Being unprotected, it perished before David found and rescued it. Even the loss of one lambs grieved his spirit, but he accepted it as a reality of life; some will perish no matter how hard we try to rescue them. David described the Lord Christ as his Shepherd.
The Lord provided his Spiritual, Physical and Material needs.

When David needed advice, food or protection from his enemies he *Walked* with the Lord Christ whom he Covenanted with. Christ gave David Physical Strength, Restoration of his Soul and Mental Fortitude, while leading him in the Paths of Righteousness in order to establish His Name with David, Israel and the heathen World.

David *Walked* side-by-side with the Lord; he didn't *Walk* before or behind but *with* the Lord Christ. This gave David spiritual courage--even to kill Goliath the Giant—a fearlessness to *Walk* in this evil world and not be afraid of the terrors that lurked in the Darkness, Evil Spirits ready to murder him---because the Rod of God protected him---just like it protected Moses. Christ's power flowed into David's life as he *Walked* in fellowship.

The Lord Jesus Christ is the Good Shepherd (John 10:11) and Christians are His sheep. We may not look like the woolly critters but our dependency on the Shepherd is the same. We need the Shepherd to anoint our heads with Oil, the Holy Spirit, to *Walk* with us like the sheep *Walked* with David.

Our food is the Word of God; His Grace is our protection from demonic and mortal predators, as we *Walk* through the Valley of the Shadow of Death, surrounded by unseen creatures waiting for an opportunity to demonically molest us; a Wicked Valley where Christians tread on vipers and scorpions --we need Him, the engrafted Word of God.

Jesus said, "I Am the Light of the World; he that follows Me shall not *Walk* in Darkness, but shall have the Light of Life" (John 8:12). Jesus is a Lamp to guide our feet and pathway.

>Luke 9:23 (KJV)
>23 "...If any man will come after Me, let him deny himself, and take up his cross daily, and follow Me."

Jesus was a Man of Purpose and Action. Wherever He went He wasted no time getting there. When He met potential disciples, He told them to set aside whatever they were doing and follow Him. On this occasion Jesus taught self-denial, the necessity and willingness to take up the Cross. He encouraged the crucifixion of the self-life, the separation from the World-Sin and the Love of Sin. This was a hard saying because it's natural to love self, family and friends.

People have been known to give their lives for family honor. How could Jesus say "deny" it all, kick everything to the curb as though it means nothing? And where will the strength to do such a feat come from?

> Luke. 14:26
> 26 If any Man come to Me, and hate not his father, and mother and wife, and children, and brethren, and sisters, yea, and hate his own [soul] life also, he cannot be My disciple."

Multitudes came to Jesus. They *Walked* with Him for various reasons; some of them conspired to crown Him their earthly King; others sought Healings and Deliverances from the torments of Sicknesses and Diseases; still others *Walked* with Him to witness signs and wonders--as though Jesus was an Entertainer.

Others *Walked* with Him because He fed them fresh fish and bread; the scribes and Pharisees *Walked* with Him to find occasion to murder Him; but the true *Walker*s came to hear and *Walk* in Agreement with the Messiah, the Word made Flesh.

At the beginning of His ministry, Jesus chose Twelve Disciples. As the Ministry progressed thousands of people wanted to become His disciples. To be His disciples meant to *Walk* with the Master in this Mortal Life and the Hereafter. Jesus shattered most of their conceptions when He told them, Verily, the way of the Cross was the initiation into His lifestyle; to hate (deny as top priority ) those dear to them. He told them this so they would count the cost whether they really wanted to be His disciples or remain in the world.

Walking with Jesus doesn't cost in a material sense but it cost in resisting the temptations of the world, living in the world but not of it. The old nature, the Sinner was Crucified, and he didn't Really want to die, but was out-voted by the rest of our being! The cost to him was devastating. This was done so the New Creature can *Walk* with Jesus.

Motives for wanting Jesus was many of His sermons. The *Appointed Destiny* Jesus wanted for their lives was more than food, popularity or Political Office: He wanted to save their Spirits, Souls and Physical Bodies to Resurrect at the Last Day. *Walking* with Jesus meant more than putting in miles on the dusty roads of Palestine.

Above all else His disciples had to trust and rest *In Him*. "Trust in the Lord with all your heart; and lean not unto your own understanding. In all your ways acknowledge Him, and He shall direct your Paths" (Proverbs 1:5,6).

Jesus also requires us to take up our Cross Daily and *Walk* in the Newness of Eternal Life (Romans 6:4). The Newness comes when we *Walk* with Him and feast upon the Word, the Bread of Life. He doesn't want lip service---all talk and no action--- or *quantity* of works, but *quality* time and Service.

Our Prayers and Meditations directed towards Him brings us closer in Covenant Relationship. For "...they that wait upon the Lord shall renew their strength; they shall mount up with wings as eagles; they shall run and not weary; and they shall *Walk* and not faint" (Isaiah 40:31). Jesus is our Rock.

Jesus took Peter, James and John atop a mountain. He didn't transport them miraculously but they *Walked* with Him. When they arrived Jesus' countenance changed: He beamed brilliantly like the star over Bethlehem the night He was born.

Moses and Elijah appeared and talked with Jesus. As the Messiah and Kinsmen Redeemer, Jesus discussed His Death, Burial and the Resurrection; He spoke on the New Testament Covenant that would be sealed in His Blood, what it meant to those in Sheol, and future generations who would *Walk* by Faith and not by sight (Luke 9:28-31).

Then a cloud overshadowed them, "and there came a voice out of the cloud, saying, This is My beloved Son; hear Him" (Luke 9: 34,35). If the disciples were too busy somewhere else to *Walk* with Jesus up the mountain, they would've missed the blessing of seeing Him Transfigure, and seeing the renown Prophets Moses and Elijah; and they would've missed hearing Jehovah-Elohim, God the Father's baritone voice--a rare occasion.

"Jesus said unto them...*Walk* while you have the Light, lest darkness come upon you; for he that *Walk* in darkness knows not whither he goes" (John 12:35). Jesus wasn't just talking about physical darkness but Spiritual Darkness too. Unless we *Walk* in the Spirit we will *Walk* in the corruption of darkness; and though we may think we know where we're going, the powers of Darkness will take us places we didn't want to go and compel us to do things we'd later be ashamed of.

Many times, especially in the wilderness, travelers who *Walk* in the darkness have actually walked off cliffs; and on many occasions travelers who Walk in the darkness have fallen into crevices, animal dens, and encountered night predators; so to *Walk* in the darkness in strange territory isn't a wise thing to do; neither is to *Walk* in the darkness of this world without Jesus, the Lamp unto our feet and a Light upon our Pathway.

Paul wrote that we should "*Walk* in the steps of Faith" Romans 4:12). Faith in Jesus Christ causes our horizons in all things to soar as we learn how to "*Walk* in Love, as Christ also has loved us, and has given Himself for us an offering and a sacrifice to God for a sweet-smelling Savoir" (Ephesians 5:1).

> Romans 5:2 (Amp. Bible)
> 2 "Through Him also we have [our] access (entrance, introduction) by Faith into this Grace (state of God's favor) in which we (firmly) *Stand*..."

**Stand With Him:** At the beginning of our journey with Jesus Christ we learned to deny ourselves and take up our Cross daily and follow Him; also to consider not the glamour of our outer appearance, worldly opinions and *Sit* at the Master's feet. We did this to be *In Christ* and receive the Inheritance appointed to the Saints, the treasures of the Kingdom of God.

At some point while hearing the Word we believed in Christ Jesus, His Deity as the Son of God. We believed via the Holy Bible that through Faith in those Holy Scriptures, the written Word of God, we became entitled to all the Promises and Provisions set forth in its sacred pages.

We asked the Lord Jesus to come into our life, and the Holy Spirit confirmed that monumental decision. We received from Him Confirmation as Born-Again Children of God.

Our relationships changed to Adoption; we were Born Again. Immediately our Human Spirit was separated from our Soul and positioned at the Throne of God. Our name was written in the Book of the Lamb that was Slain.

Not only were we spiritually separated but also mentally severed from the bondages of the world powers, the Rulers of the Darkness of this age who use the Law of Sin and Death. Now we must *Walk* in the Spirit, abide in the Life of Christ within us to benefit from this separation. Faith-reckoning in the crucifixion of Jesus Christ activates the separation from the world powers.

> Ephesians 6:12 (Amp. Bible)
> 12 For we are not wrestling with flesh and blood [contending only with physical opponents], but against the Despotisms, against the Powers, against [the Master Spirits who are] the World Rulers of this present Darkness, against the spirit forces of wickedness in the heavenly sphere."

As the Holy Spirit impresses upon our Human Spirit the Surpassing Greatness of our Savior and His Plans, Purposes and Pursuits, we came to realize the Spiritual Warfare involved in keeping His Presence among us and our Soul in our Destiny.

God's enemy became our enemy; but God through Jesus Christ defeated Satan at Calvary; therefore God's victory is ours too! As the Redeemed by the Blood, it's our duty to *Stand* on that victory and live the victorious lives as Kings and Priests of the Living Christ.

Our Faith has brought us into Grace wherewith we *Stand* upon what we Believe is Truth about our Savior. It's He who empowers us to *Stand* before Him and against Satan's schemes.

We are Commanded to be strong in the Lord; this is accomplished through our *Stand*, our Righteousness, Right-Relationship nurtured throughout the years. We draw our strength and battlefield tactics and armor from His Holy Spirit; who like a flood rushes forth and destroys the yokes of Demonic Bondages whenever and wherever they materialize.

We're heavily armed with Spiritual Weapons activated by a push of our Faith Button. We're more than able to weather the storms; we have God on our side.

The Word states that our warfare isn't against other Human Beings but against the Rulers and Spiritual Forces of Wickedness in the heavenly spheres.

Many Christian "Religious" Leaders deny the existence of these forces—they Preach and Teach everything else but avoid talking about Demons--yet the Holy Bible is well written on the subject of Satan and his Fallen Angels.

Many Christian Theologians disagree or minimize the direct participation, interference or effects of the wickedness perpetrated in the world by this unseen army. Therefore, the Evil that is perpetrated under the sun goes unchallenged (but not always unnoticed) by them. They believe the majority of world problems are Manmade and one day Man will mature and outgrow them.

Many believe that Sickness, Poverty, Calamity and Tragedy are the results of Karma, Fate, Faithlessness, Personal Sins, the Act or will of God--when often it's Demonic Oppression and our ignorance in spiritual matters to Keep Demons in check. Spiritual Warfare is taught not inherited.

The same group of well-meaning Christians minimize who we are in the grand stage of life: To them, we're the helpless, broken-down, "declawed" and passive people who can't wait to die and go to Heaven. No! We're the Lord's Special Forces, the Elite Soldiers patrolling the Spiritual and Physical Realms. We're the Lord's Army, empowered by Jesus Christ to *Stand* and Occupy until He returns. We could be the last occupying force.

As the Lord's Special Forces we're not looking for confrontations with Man or Demons; but we take care of business when Demons come knocking at our door. We hold our ground and administer the Yoke-Destroying, Burden-Bearing, Devil-Stomping Anointing of Himself ministering through us into Creation.

> Matthew 20:1,3,4 (KJV)
> 1 "For the Kingdom of Heaven is like unto a Man that is an householder, which went out early in the morning to hire laborers into his vineyard. 3 And he went out about the third hour, and saw others Standing idle in the marketplace. 4 And said unto them, Go into the vineyard, and whatsoever is right I will give you."

As Un-Regenerated Man, the Spiritually Walking and Talking Dead, we were *Standing* around, spiritually idle. In the natural it appeared we were living a full life, moving along at a fast pace with the rest of the Walking and Talking Dead World. Some of us were speeding recklessly through life, needing mental and physical repairs and without good brakes or judgment.

Nevertheless to God we were *Standing* idle, not serving Him in the Vineyard of Creation. The Holy Spirit pulled us over and arrested us. He charged us as habitual, spiritual criminals—and would have locked us up and thrown away the key---but Jesus paid the price for our immediate release and freedom.

God sent His Son into Creation to save Sinners from the wages of our Sins which is Death. Now, at this final hour before

Jesus returns, God *Walks* to and fro throughout the Earth looking for laborers for the End Time Harvest of Souls.

The Lord supplies all the necessary tools and equipment to work in His Vineyard. He chose the Gifts and Callings. All we have to do is show up for work. God said whatever is right He will pay; and God is the best Paymaster!

The first shall be last and the last shall be first; there's no seniority among labors The main thing is that we cease to *Stand* idle in the world and *Stand* busy for God. He's the true owner of the Vineyard: Creation and Man, the grapes, are His. But a scandalous thief, Satan stole Creation and Man from Adam.

Creation and the people in it are His Vineyard, and it's most extraordinary; it's in the Vineyard that the Spiritual Adoptions take place; it's here Spiritual Warfare is learned; it's the Divine Boot Camp for training His Special Forces to fight the Wars of the Lord. It's in the Vineyard where we learn how to take orders from our Commander-in-Chief, Jesus Christ the Righteous.

It's also in the Vineyard where we learn the Spiritual M.A.S.H. procedures--how to Pray the Prayer of Faith to Heal the Sick and bind up the emotionally wounds. It's in the Vineyard that we learn how to master the various Defensive and Offensive Spiritual Weapons and Weapon Systems: Love, Joy, Peace, Goodness, Patience, Self-Control...the Fruit of the Spirit.

It's where the Weapon Systems, Spiritual Gifts are honed. In the Vineyard we master the Sword of the Spirit, the Word of God, and the Shield of Faith. We have become more than conquers as a New Species of Life!

The *Wonderful Destiny* we have involves *change*. This *change* the Holy Spirit has for us isn't always from the inside out but also from the outside in. He uses the Environment of the Vineyard to touch us and effect lasting *changes*.

The Environmental sections of the Vineyard are our home, church, school, job, social place, hospital, street, prison, Jail, Rehabilitation Center, Institution—wherever we are, the Holy Spirit can use it to teach us something Eternal.

All Creation belongs to the Lord. He uses each environment to bring the desirable *change*s. Each environment the Spirit of God touches our souls and flesh to teach us. He destroys Addictions, removes Character Flaws, corrects Sinful Behaviors and other undesirables traits.

His interactions with our Environment is to change us by subtracting the things we don't need, the burdens binding us to slavery, the carnality that's making our Spiritual Journey difficult. He shakes loose all those things until what's left is Christ-Like Behavior, Personality and Service.

"And we know that all things work together for the *good* to them that Love God, to them who are the called according to His Purpose" (Romans 8:28). So the *good* works for the *good* and the bad works for the *good*--according to His purpose. God uses Environment, Circumstances, Situations, Trials and Tribulations to teach us Spiritual Lessons.

Jesus of Nazareth was "*predestinated to be conformed* to the image of His Son, that He might be the first born among many brethren" (Romans 8:29). We forget that the Spirit of God had to work inside the Man Jesus to *conform* Him to be Lord, Christ, the Son of God in the flesh; the Holy Spirit also worked Environmentally in His life.

"Though He was a Son, yet *learned He Obedience by the things which He suffered*" (Hebrews 5:8). Suffering can be spiritual, mental and physical anguish. Jesus was born and raised in a religious and hostile environment: Herod the Great tried to kill Him at His birth. In His youth and adulthood He dealt with the Sanhedrin Council, Romans, crime, poverty, sickness and general Demonic Oppression over Israel. We can reason that He learned many things while living there Thirty-Three Years.

So we know that Environment plays an important part in our being *conformed* into the image of Jesus Christ, because it played an important part in Him being *conformed*; being tempted by Satan and the seductions of the world, He overcame them to become our Understanding and Merciful High Priest. It stands to reason the more we know about the Holy Spirit's Ministry in our Environment, and us--the Visible and Invisible Realms, the better Christian Soldiers we'll become.

> John 15:1,16 (NIV)
> 1 "I Am the True Vine, and My Father is the Gardener.
> 16 You did not choose Me, but I *Chose and Appointed* you to go and bear fruit."

The Vineyard, within the Creation Environment is where the True Vine flourishes. The Father is the Gardener who owns and oversees the productivity of the Vine.

We as Christians are the Branches connected and depended on the True Vine for our existence, nourishment and resistance to diseases. We didn't create or chose the Vine, but Jehovah-Elohim the Gardener planted the True Vine, Jesus Christ, in the moist earth; and when the fullness of the time arrived, the True Vine emerged from the earth, and chose us to bear His Fruit.

The Branches produce Fruit as a direct results of the strength of the Vine. Therefore if the True Vine doesn't produce adequate Fruit, the Branches are pruned (cleansed from corruption) to comply with the needs of the Gardener. The Gardener has. a "green thumb" when it comes to maintaining the Vine and His Branches.

> Genesis 41:38  50:20 (NIV)
> 38 "So Pharaoh asked them, Can we find anyone like this man, one in whom is the Spirit of God? 20 You intended to harm me, but God intended it for good to accomplish what is now being done, the saving of many lives."

The life of Joseph bears record to the necessity to Stand with God and how environment was used in for his life. The Holy Spirit showed Joseph two visions: The first was as the youngest son, he would have Authority over his brothers. The second vision showed Joseph with Authority over his parents. Joseph was only a seventeen year old shepherd boy when the Spirit revealed his *Destiny*.

These two visions revealed the climax of his life achievements. But Joseph became lifted up with a Spirit of Pride; he became arrogant, abusive and uncaring about the feelings of others. The visions went to his head, plus he was Jacob's favorite son. So to make matters worse, Jacob made Joseph a multi-colored coat.

Joseph's older brothers already hated his guts because of the special treatment Joseph received. So when Joseph told them the first vision, his eleven brothers would be in obeisance to him, they wanted to wring his neck!

"...the sun and the moon and the eleven stars made obeisance to me...and his father rebuked him, and said, What is this dream that you have dreamed? Shall I and your mother and your brethren indeed come to bow ourselves to you to the earth?" (Genesis 37:9,10). That boy had a lot of explaining to do.

Joseph was overconfident in his native Environment. He disregarded the culture and traditions of respect and humility in dealing with his parents and elder brothers. The proper thing for him was to have kept the visions to himself until the Holy Spirit advised him differently. The temptation to lift himself up above others became unbearable. Satan was at work in his life.

One day Israel (Jacob) sent Joseph to find his brothers. When his brothers saw him they sighed bitterly, "Behold, this dreamer comes" (v.19). At first they decided to kill Joseph and throw his corpse into a pit, afterwards tell their father a wild beast killed and ate him.

But Ruben, the elder brother (who had Authority over all the brothers) said no--don't kill him but cast him into a pit. He hoped to come back later and rescue him. Yet Ruben left and when Joseph arrived they stripped him of his "love" coat and cast him into an empty pit.

As they sat around eating and considering what to do with the "dreamer", a company of Ishmaelite, Midianite merchantmen stopped on their way to Egypt. Dollar signs showed in the brother's eye sockets. They sold Joseph for twenty pieces of silver (v.28).

Ruben returned to the pit and Joseph was gone. The brethren took Joseph's coat, dipped it in goat's blood and brought it to Israel. The sight of the bloody coat broke Israel's heart and he mourned grievously. Of course, Ruben went along with the revised plan. He probably got a cut of the money.

The Midianites sold Joseph to Potiphar, the Captain (and Chief Executioner) of Pharaoh's Guard. In this Environment Joseph's *Destiny* began to unfold. Certainly the Lord was with him in the pit and now in Egypt.

He learned respect and responsibility, financial management and labor relations. He prospered in everything he set his mind to. He also learned to Praise and Worship the Lord God; and God Fellowshipped and *Stood* by him.

Potiphar recognized the Spirit of God working with Joseph and Joseph found Grace in the eyes of this powerful Egyptian. He made Joseph Overseer of his entire household. Potiphar was blessed because Joseph was present in his house: "And the blessing of the Lord was upon all that he had in the house, and in the field" (Genesis 39:5). Joseph was wise and prudent.

Then a Spirit of Lust possessed Potiphar's wife. She saw the handsome, muscular Israelite and she tried to seduce Joseph: "Lie with me," she pleaded.

Joseph refused and tried to reason with her. Potiphar was good to him; he trusted Joseph with everything--including his wife. "How then can I do this great wickedness, and sin against God?"(v.9). This temporarily appeased her sexual advances.

This new Environment changed Joseph's concept of life which included concern for how God views his actions.

But while Joseph thought upon this new predicament, the Evil Spirit torment Potiphar's wife until Joseph was all she could think about. That lusty Demon drove her insane with passion. In her delusions she thought Joseph played hard to get. She waited and stalked him with her eyes. She saw him come into the house and wanted him even more than before. She caught him by the garment and pulled him close. She snarled, "Lie with me!"

Joseph slipped out of his garment and ran out the house! Furious at not being gratified, she called the servants and showed them Joseph's garment, telling them he tried to rape her.

When Potiphar found out he was angry yet perplexed. He thought he knew Joseph, that the Spirit of the Lord was with him and caused his household to prosper; but the accusation of his wife couldn't be ignored; though he knew she was lying.

If Potiphar didn't do something it implied he knew she lied, or he didn't really love her. He couldn't appear to others as weak; but if he executed Joseph on her word and he wasn't guilty, the God whom Joseph Worshipped surely would bring calamity upon him.; and afterwards Potiphar wouldn't have two sticks to rub together, providing he was still breathing!

He couldn't free Joseph because people would talk. So the safest thing to do was send Joseph to prison, where the King's prisoners were kept.

In this new Environment the Lord was still with Joseph. He gave him Special Grace in the sight of the Keeper of the prison. The Keeper committed to Joseph all the prisoners. Even the Keeper of the prison realized the Spirit of the Lord was with Joseph though he was in prison accused of Attempted Rape.

Joseph prospered in his Environment and learned many new things, spiritual lessons such as Integrity, Sensitivity, Patience, Humility, Mercy, Grace, Kindness and Forgiveness.

Before leaving home he was selfish and hurtful to those around him. Now he was changed: He saw visions and interpreted dreams for the Guards and Prisoners.

Joseph had the first Prison Ministry. He ministered to the higher echelon of Egyptian Officials who were imprisoned or on Official Business. Perhaps he converted some of the heathen, Idol Worshippers, Magicians, Astrologers and Pagan Philosophers.

People that Joseph helped promise to help him out of his situation, but when released they forgot about him. But Joseph didn't despair because his Hope was in God and not men. He continued to Praise and Worship God.

One night the Lord gave Pharaoh two disturbing dreams that none of his Counselors, Wise Men and Astrologers could interpret. Then the Spirit of the Lord caused the Chief Butler to remember Joseph; Satan caused the Butler to forget humble Joseph. The Butler told Pharaoh about the Anointed Hebrew locked away in prison.

Soon Joseph was before Pharaoh and accurately interpreted the dreams: There would be Seven Years of plenty followed by Seven Years of famine. Joseph also advised Pharaoh on how to manage the resources to offset the years of famine. Pharaoh was impressed!

> Genesis 41:38,40 (KJV)
> 38 "And Pharaoh said unto his servants, Can we find such a one as this, a Man whom the Spirit of God is?
> 40 You shall be over my house, and according to your word shall my people be ruled..."

Joseph was Thirty Years Old when he became Governor in Egypt. He was Seventeen Years Old when his brothers sold him into slavery. Joseph served Eleven Years as Potiphar's servant and then Two years in prison.

He went from the Pit to Potiphar; from Potiphar to Prison, and from Prison to the Palace. Through it all the *changes* in his life came through his Environments.

Joseph learned Obedience by the things that he suffered: To serve God and others. No longer did he think only of himself but the good of Humanity. He got the victory in every situation and Environment he encountered.

It would've been easier for him to have given up at the turn of events in his prideful life; but he *Stood* upon the Promises contained in the Visions, the Word of God revealed a greater good would emerge from the ashes of an apparent defeat. He knew in his heart the Word would prevail.

Of course the famine arrived as scheduled and it reached Canaan where Israel and his sons were. So Israel sent his sons to Egypt to buy food. They didn't know that Joseph was Governor in Egypt, and they had to deal directly with him.

"And Joseph's brethren came, and bowed down themselves before him with their faces to the earth" (Genesis 42:6). After telling them who he was, Joseph sent for the whole family: "And Joseph placed his father and his brethren, and gave them a possession in the land of Egypt...And Joseph nourished his father, and his brethren...(Genesis 47:11,12). "

Indeed the whole family depended on Joseph in whom the Spirit of God used to save the people.

The Lord Jesus Christ desires to work "all things together" for the good in our many Environments. There's something for us to learn in every situation; we must Stand with him.

## *New Testament Covenant Prayers*

He is the Holy Spirit who helps us to pray according to the Will of God. The Holy Spirit used the Apostle Paul to pray into the earth the Father's will concerning His Spiritual Children:

> Adapted from Colossians 1:9-14
> 9 "For this reason, since the day we heard about you, we have not stopped praying for you and asking God to fill you with Knowledge of His Will through all Spiritual Wisdom and Understanding. 10 And we Pray in order that you may live a life worthy of the Lord and may please Him in every way; bearing Fruit in every good work, growing in the Knowledge of God, 11 being strengthened with all Power according to His Glorious Might so that you may have great Endurance and Patience, and joyfully,

12 giving thanks to the Father, who has qualified you to share in the Inheritance of the Saints of the Kingdom of Light. 13 For He has rescued us from the Dominion of Darkness and brought us into the Kingdom of the Son He loves, 14 in whom we have Redemption, the Forgiveness of Sins.

Adapted from Ephesians 1:17-20 2:6
17 "I keep asking that the God of our Lord Jesus Christ, the Glorious Father, may give you the Spirit of Wisdom and Revelation, so that you may know Him better. 18 I Pray also that the eyes of your heart may be enlightened in order that you may know the Hope to which He has Called you, the riches of His Glorious Inheritance in the Saints, 19 and His incomparably Great Power for us who Believe. That Power is like the working of His Mighty Strength, 20 which He exerted in Christ when He raised Him from the dead and Seated Him at His Right Hand in the Heavenly Realms. 6 And God raised us up with Christ and Seated us with Him in the Heavenly Realms In Christ Jesus.

Adapted From Ephesians 3:16-19
16 I Pray that out of His Glorious Riches He may strengthen you with Power through His Spirit in your Inner Being, 17 so that Christ may dwell in your hearts through Faith. And I pray that you, being rooted and established in Love, 18 may have Power, together with all the Saints, to grasp how wide and long and high and deep is the Love of Christ, 19 and to know this Love that surpasses Knowledge--that you may be filled to the Measure of all the Fullness of God."

The Destiny of Man is to be filled to the Measure with Christ. Forever seek your Appointed Destiny.

www.ingramcontent.com/pod-product-compliance
Lightning Source LLC
LaVergne TN
LVHW051101080426
835508LV00019B/2001